Stephen,
    This comes w
you made in my
cross style conferences you ...
I pray that the Lord will continue to bless
you and Delphine as you lead others to serve
in the kingdom.
                        Shirley

Riding In Cars
With Men

Shirley M. Goodman

To download a free group discussion guide, visit

www.shirleygoodman.com

Riding In Cars With Men: A Clergywoman's Story

Copyright © 2019 TheSheRev, LLC

All rights reserved.

All Scripture quotations, unless otherwise indicated, are taken from the Holy Bible, *New International Version®, NIV®*. Copyright © 1973, 1978, 1984, 2011 by Biblica, Inc.™ Used by permission of Zondervan. All rights reserved worldwide. **www.zondervan.com**.

The "NIV" and "New International Version" are trademarks registered in the United States Patent and Trademark Office by Biblica, Inc.

ISBN: 978-1-7337433-0-3

eBook ISBN:978-1-7337433-1-0

DEDICATION

This book is dedicated first and foremost to the Lord Jesus Christ who, by his death and resurrection, provided for our salvation. His free grace and unconditional love completely transformed my life.

To Ron, my amazing husband and best friend on this earth, who continues to faithfully live this journey with me.

To all the clergywomen of the past who paved the way for us, and the many women who presently live with a call to ministry and are forging into the future with holy optimism and zeal.

To both my male and female mentors, advocates, colleagues and friends who have shared this ride with me.

*"Let us hold unswervingly to the hope we profess,
for he who promised is faithful."*
Hebrews 10:23

TABLE OF CONTENTS

PREFACE

Every clergy person has his or her own story.

This is simply a part of mine.

It reflects experiences, insights and ideas about what my journey has been like as a woman in a male-dominated vocation. It's about working relationships between male and female clergy. It's about the connection with God's people in the church and my role as a pastor.

I will share with you how my life has been redeemed and transformed by the love of Christ and His saving power. I'll explain how God placed a call to ministry on my life, and tell the story of my response as one of many who have heard this call.

When I started down this road as a pastor and preacher, I couldn't have anticipated the amazing direction my call would take over the next 25 years. I have loved every assignment, and each one had its ups and downs.

The people of the church have loved me, admonished me, loved some more, discipled me, loved again, and nurtured me into a deep faith in God. And the Holy Spirit continues to mold and shape my heart as I desire to be formed into the image of Christ.

It's often said that vocational ministry is a marathon, not a sprint. The called ones are in it for the duration. It is an extremely thrilling journey. But, like most things in life, it can also be painful and difficult at times, even in the church where we expect to be safe.

Telling my story in print has prompted me to choose excerpts from the wonderful and not-so-wonderful experiences I've had as a minister. My hope is to give voice to the experiences of many other clergywomen who have faced the same hurdles – ones that may have prohibited them from fully employing their call. There are many who still feel left out of the inner circle fueled by the systems in which they operate.

For the clergywomen who are gainfully employed or engaged in ministry that meets their calling, I ask that you would remember to encourage your sisters by becoming models, champions and mentors. You represent to the larger context of the church what ministering as a clergywoman is all about.

Work for the Lord to the best of your ability. Confront injustice or other issues that infect mutual relationships. Let your male counterparts learn from you as you learn from them. Establish collegial relationships that advance the kingdom. Remain humble yet proud. Help others gain understanding of your position and place by remaining open, vulnerable, positive and hopeful.

If you are a male clergyperson or lay leader in the church, I offer an insider's view of what it can be like to work with you and how we can be more effective together. You will read about people and situations that include a combination of joy and sadness, even injustice. They represent the need for both personal and systemic change.

Regardless of gender, we can all pray for transformation by the Holy Spirit – transformation that creates dialogue and then goes beyond to practices that are equal for men and women in ministry. While it's beginning to happen in some places, the response is slow when compared to the urgency of the need.

Each of us – male or female – can either hinder or help.

The choice is ours.

I truly believe that things will change in time because we are part of the solution.

Riding in Cars with Men offers honest insight to some of my real experiences as a pastor. I hope that it will equip, enlighten, and encourage you. If just one person is motivated by my story to accept women in ministry as Biblically called equals, then progress has been made.

I wish you prayerful reading and spirit filled conversation.

There are far, far better things ahead
than any we leave behind.

- C.S. Lewis

CHAPTER 1

THE JOURNEY BEGINS

Culture shock.

There's no better way to describe how I felt.

It was at a conference where, over lunch, several pastors were sitting at a table with me. The conversation drifted into a discussion over issues related to how men and women work together in ministry. That's when one of my male colleagues said something like this:

If I found one of my male associate pastors riding with a woman in his car for any reason, I would fire him on the spot.

I was stunned and appalled by the firmness of this blatant declaration. But looking back, I now realize his statement and my reaction had something to do with a difference in our cultures, a word that is defined as "the set of shared attitudes, values, goals, and practices that characterizes an institution or organization."[1] Culture shows itself in how people behave and what habits they have or paradigms they hold. And it may include attitudes they have toward one another or others outside their culture.

For me, coming into ministry was a lot like driving a car for the first time in South Africa. Yes, it's a car. From the outside, it looks just like the ones in the United States. But once you get inside, everything in front of you emerges from an entirely different vantage point.

It's awkward to sit in the driver's seat on the opposite side, and it requires careful attention to detail in order to identify and stay in the correct lane, especially when you're turning corners. The experience reorients you in a profound way.

Yes, it's still driving, but in a very different context. It feels strange, fun and scary all at the same time. That's how entering full-time pastoral ministry felt to me.

Anyone entering a new culture can experience lots of emotion, frustration and adjustment before they are able to adapt, as someone who made the choice to live in a foreign country can tell you. But there's no need to actually travel so far if you want to experience all that for yourself.

In my case, no passport or visa was required. All it took was a career switch.

My cultural background at work began in business organizations far away from the insiders' world of ministry. For over 18 years, I earned my living in the corporate world of sales and marketing. And in that environment, men and women traveled together regularly, including across the country. Lunches, dinners and all kinds of meeting scenarios were a normal part of work.

For six years, I owned and operated a sales and marketing consultancy, which had me traveling locally and nationally to client sites, trade shows and association meetings. That entire time, my closest colleague was a man. So there were countless hours spent in the car together as we rode from state to state to meet with customers, and speak at or lead workshops at trade shows. There was also time spent in the office alone discussing clients and programs, and flights to and from cities across the country. Yet never once was there anything other than a collegial relationship.

Ours was always a "brother and sister" connection. Both Christians, we actually spent a lot of time together talking about how God was shaping us in life. We came at many issues from different theological points of view, and it was often on those rides in the car that we listened, questioned, debated and challenged each other.

They were sacred times and, since both of us would eventually leave the corporate world and become ministers, I genuinely think those talks helped shape our call to ministry, especially since we came from different church traditions.

In my college cross-cultural classes, I was taught that we don't recognize culture until we bump into it. I quickly learned the profound truth of that when I entered into my new vocation of ministry. The cultural norms in this male-dominated environment were very different than what I experienced back in the regular realm of business. In so many ways and at so many times, it felt like we were speaking completely different languages with completely different worldviews.

It was culture shock, pure and simple.

Culture shock occurs when someone suddenly steps into a set of unexpected experiences in a cultural setting other than their own. The symptoms include confusion, anxiety and/or dissonance, and these feelings will continue until the newcomer can accept or at least work within the customs and mores of his or her new setting.

At some point, the person will either positively or negatively adapt to the new culture. They may even decide whether to stay or leave. But before that point, there's a sense of being lost while familiar "norms" are completely rearranged, or discarded and replaced with new ones, including various customs that can be hard to comprehend or apply. No matter what good intentions a person has going into the experience, they may not expect it to be so different. And it takes a while to adapt.

For me, the culture clash I experienced going into ministry wasn't a mere "bump." It was more like a front-end collision!

Being a first-generation member in my denomination, I didn't grow up with some of the thinking that others took, and still take, for granted. I never heard of the "Billy Graham Rule" nor anticipated the passion that some have for certain understood lines of propriety between the sexes.

But on that fateful day in that eye-opening conversation, I began to learn how seriously some take those cultural rules, including the following:

- ✓ You cannot ride alone in a car with a person of the opposite sex.
- ✓ You must have all your meetings out in public.

✓ There must always be someone else in the building if a man and woman are there alone.

✓ There must be a window in every office.

✓ Don't go into a man's house or let him into yours unless someone else is present (e.g. spouse, children, etc.).

And the list goes on.

While I understood the intentions behind those ideas, I was baffled – and on some counts, just plain angry. That's why I spoke up to my colleague that day.

"You make it sound like men can't control themselves. Like, at any opportunity, they can't keep their pants zipped. And while I understand your concerns about guidelines and accountability, I don't understand the severity of your opinion here. Fire someone? Really?"

I reminded him that my best female friend and I had traveled the country together, sharing rooms, cars and other experiences. "In this day," I told him, "we could be labeled as lesbians because we travel together. Does that mean we should stop? Should we lose our jobs?"

That left him speechless for a minute, pausing the conversation as I realized he wasn't ready for my seemingly unpastoral comments. Fortunately, we were able to continue the dialogue to a mutual "agree to disagree" close in the end.

Even so, I just didn't get it. My cultural norms of how to do business were turned upside down when I entered the ministry. Interestingly enough, in part because the female friend I referred to was single at the time, she held more of my male colleague's view than mine. She didn't ride in cars with men alone, proof that even clergywomen approach this subject differently. And because she's someone I respect deeply, knowing her position forced me to think about my own understanding of the matter even further.

I did and still do want to be cautiously wise about such interactions. I understand that things sometimes happen that no one ever thought would. I'm not naïve, and I do realize there can be temptation. But I believe that people who might succumb to temptation, especially sexual, will do so with or without these rules. Headlines recounting the fall of otherwise strong Christian leaders tell me this is true. So, based on the arguments laid out for me, I'm not convinced that these well-meaning guidelines will make much difference. And my previous positive experiences working with men reinforce that belief.

I am also convinced that the church should be a place that models healthy relationships between the sexes rather than encouraging us to simply avoid each other (more on this later). So, all this left me wondering what I should do to be respectful of those who didn't share my point of view when I still had so many unanswered questions.

Did this belief mean that I couldn't have my biological brother come into the house to visit me if I was home alone? How far does one take this "rule"? Can we always "avoid the appearance of evil" (the justification given to me) when we know that people's minds can bend toward evil anyway, leaving them to think what they want to think no matter the truth? How are we to manage the real circumstances pastors face in the day-to-day life of ministry?

I needed a way to handle this new paradigm.

Ultimately, I made an agreement with my husband that, if he knew where I was and who I was with – and if a male travelling companion was married, and his wife knew where he was and who he was with – it was okay to proceed. Of course, this also required sensitivity to the Spirit, but it worked for me. And I have to tell you again – *I've had some phenomenal spiritual conversations riding in cars with men.*

Now let me back up a minute. In case you're unfamiliar with the Billy Graham rule, famed evangelist Rev. Dr. William Graham gets credit for its origination; thus the name. In the 1940s, he established the rule that he would never be alone with a woman other than his wife. He and his team traveled extensively to promote the gospel, and it's understandable why he would create a boundary like this to protect his integrity as a minister.

It's important to note, however, that the role of women in the 1940s was very different than it is today. Women are now integrated into every phase of professional life, whether ministry or business. To get things done, to make decisions, to strategize and plan, it's inevitable that a situation will occur when a man and a woman find themselves alone together.

While the implication is that men must protect themselves from sexual temptation and women must be kept at a distance to do so, the consequences have to be taken into consideration too. Because that means women can be left out of the many informal networks and places where decisions are made – based on the best intentions or not. What gets lost is our input and influence to the way business is done and conclusions are drawn. And there can be an information gap, compared to our male peers, in what we need to know to do our jobs well.

Even more difficult to contend with is the message of fear that's communicated by some people who employ this rule: that women are a *de facto* sexual threat to their male colleagues.

Which is wrong.

Or that men are incapable of avoiding temptations.

Which is also wrong.

Both ideas undermine the biblical truth that clearly states that both men and women are made in the image of God. And both genders are capable of avoiding – or yielding to – temptation of any kind. Scripture tells us that those who walk in the Spirit will live by the Spirit and thus will choose what is righteous and holy.

But Scripture also tells us that our enemy, the devil, is a liar. He is wily and roams around in this fallen world, looking for someone to devour. So, if following God's Word is a real priority for Christian people, again, I think this makes the rules unwarranted, especially in the way they have been applied in the church.

Merianna Harrelson, pastor of New Hope Christian Fellowship in West Columbia, South Carolina, said she first encountered the Billy Graham Rule in youth group when she was encouraged to turn to female interns for counseling or advice instead of her male youth minister. "I can remember thinking that there was something more going on in the interactions the male youth group members were getting that I wasn't receiving because they had access to the youth minister," she said.

Harrelson said the idea that professional adults need chaperones "perpetuates false notions of sexuality."

"Men are not sexual beings who cannot control their sexual desires," she said. "Females are not sexual temptresses. When we operate in the adult, professional world with these false, negative ideas of sexuality, we only reinforce a culture of sexual abuse, sexual harassment and spiritual abuse."[2] And we also reinforce a culture that disenfranchises women because they are women.

It's likely that a female pastor will end up visiting men at the hospital the same way a male pastor may have to visit a woman. They will be asked to counsel men at church the same way a male pastor will be asked to counsel women. The male janitor will come to clean before they leave work for the day. They may ride with colleagues for long distances to training classes or for meetings. And while each of these scenarios may require appropriate boundaries, it's unnecessary and unwise to create a culture of anxiety.

We ought to operate out of wisdom, not fear.

Yet I have met male ministers who seem to live in fear of being seen with a woman alone. And while I respect their right to hold this view, I do not agree that it's a healthy one. There has to be a better way for us to work together.

A few years ago, I gave a ride to a male colleague so that his wife could keep the car home to run the kids around. We were going to a weekend training event that was about two hours away, and both of our spouses were okay with this arrangement. I've been a friend of this younger-than-me man for many years, and we had a great time throwing around ideas and chewing on spiritual truths.

On the way home, we had one of the most amazing conversations about a very controversial topic, where we discovered that we didn't agree at all on how to interpret Scripture or apply it to today's culture, even though we were of the same theological bent. The result was a lively discussion that challenged both of our thinking.

7

While some may have thought it wrong for us to ride together, I was so glad for that time of conversation! It helped shape both of us. That's the kind of interaction I'm talking about when I say that caution is one thing and common sense is another. I've twice had male associate pastors working on my staff where we negotiated appropriate boundaries all the time, even though I was clearly old enough to be their mother.

With that said, if you find yourself on a staff or team that includes both men and women, I suggest setting aside time to discuss what kind of boundaries are best for your team and what the implications are for everyone involved. Engage your spouses too, if applicable, if that will help. Work out and agree on a plan that insures your working relationship is designed with parameters that work for everyone affected.

This might also include boundaries for phone, text, email or other electronic forms of communication that are now invaluable resources for connecting. I once heard of a female pastor who had to have a conversation with the wife of one of her ministry leaders because she was upset that her husband was receiving texts at home from the pastor. These things do happen.

So, establish guidelines and let others in the church, especially church leaders, know what the plan is. This will help answer questions before they're asked and give parameters that everyone understands and agrees on. Then watch for how the plan works and adjust it accordingly. This allows you to be proactive in setting the rules of propriety for your team or ministry. It may also include what time of day is okay to contact each other and what the rules are for texting on the staff's days off, vacations or designated family time.

To adapt effectively to this ministry culture, it's amazing how much I've had to learn through intuition: watching, listening and emulating what the men did, translating all the while through my female lens and making sure to retain my gender distinctive.

It's probably important to mention here that men were the only pastoral models I had when I came into ministry. I joined a district of

66 churches, and I was aware of only one other clergywoman besides me. She lived about 4 1/2 hours away from where I served, so we never met. I had no other female figures in my network to look to as readily available mentors or role models, only men. As a result, there were times I felt very alone.

Not long ago, I took a Strengths Finder train-the-trainer class. In a mock interview before the class, I mentioned that my "strategic" strength has often left me feeling lonely in ministry. That surprised the coach, and he wanted to know more. So I told him that, as a leader, I often instinctively know which way to move forward, but I can't always explain it to other people because all the details aren't clear yet. That leaves me feeling alone in the vision and how to execute it.

He raised his eyebrows at that. "I can't say I've ever felt lonely in ministry."

This from a man who has served much longer than I have! It was as intriguing a response to me as mine had been to him. For his part, he said that he worked closely with a male colleague who had strategic strengths, and now he wondered if that man ever felt alone like I did. I too would be interested to know if some of my male counterparts with strategic gifts have felt alone like me.

One way or the other, several weeks after the class was over, I was thinking about his remarks and realized that my being a *female* visionary leader adds to my sense of aloneness. Which means it was likely even more difficult for the women who came before me in ministry.

Many people just don't know what to do with a woman who follows her instincts to lead. Some consider it to be "touchy-feely." But that's not necessarily true. In my case at least, it's a strategic strength at work. I'm good at sifting through various possibilities in a given situation to determine the best way to move forward toward specific, structural goals. Some have welcomed such input. Other times, my natural and honed abilities were dismissed based on gender.

In the church and as comrades in ministry, I've found that many clergymen simply don't see how the network they've established is very closed to women. It's a culture unto itself. On one occasion, I jokingly greeted a female colleague at her ordination interview with the words, "Welcome to the club!" since I was the only other woman in the room of about 20 people. Immediately, a deep gasp erupted from one of the men, and I got a subtle scolding as if what I'd said wasn't the truth.

But it was.

These wonderful, godly men – many of whom I consider good friends – can't understand what it's like to walk into the room and be evaluated by 20 men and just one woman. Or worse, no women at all. Somehow, even in that environment, we're supposed to feel a collegial camaraderie that often doesn't exist.

I'm so appreciative of the men who are sensitive to their female counterparts and who try to create a more welcoming environment. In my experience, it is getting better.

But we still have a long way to go.

CHAPTER 2

WHICH WAY DO WE GO?

Navigating your way through a new city or town may require a map or GPS to successfully get where you're going. We have to discover which are the best main roads, where the side roads take you, and how to avoid accidents or even detours.

But there's no GPS for relationships. You're on your own, finding your way as you go.

I understood right away that I would need to find creative ways to adapt to the new culture I found myself operating in, specifically in regard to how men and women do or don't work together in ministry. This was all so new to me.

One of the ways I adapted early on was to look for the positives of working together rather than the negatives. For instance, I decided to make the most of being the only woman at pastoral events. I would purposefully look for things to celebrate. For example, I used to joke that going to events hosted by our district was one of the few places I didn't have to wait in line at the ladies' room!

I'm happy to say that's no longer the case. There are a lot more women of various ages serving in ministry around me now, so that bathroom line is growing. But in the beginning, it definitely wasn't something I even thought about expecting or not expecting.

Oddly enough, even the idea that I was out of place was a learning experience for me. Because working with men was what I knew best, it initially felt comfortable – I just had no idea how uncomfortable it was for them. For my part, I grew up with two brothers and no sisters, so my orientation toward life naturally leans toward a male understanding of how things work. As such, I've been told more often than I can count how I'm "just like one of the guys."

Already knowing that he meant it as a compliment, I once asked a male pastor friend of mine, "What do you really mean when you say that?"

"It's like saying, 'You're in!'" he explained. "I think of it like a brotherhood, and you're included. You're an insider. I can be raw and real with you. I can punch you in the arm (figuratively speaking). Not all women are comfortable being around men, but you don't adjust who you are, and I don't have to edit myself to be accepted."

Now, this friend was a police officer before he entered the ministry, so I totally understood his reference to "brotherhood." My husband had been a union carpenter for years: the "brotherhood of carpenters." So that clarification allowed me to better interpret what was meant. And yes, from my friend, this was a compliment and I received it as such.

Nonetheless, while I'm glad to be included in the "brotherhood," the reality is – no! I'm not one of the guys! I think, dress, listen and express myself differently. I'm a woman with a valuable perspective to offer – one that isn't always easily heard.

Once again, more about that later though...

Over the years, I've learned a lot about how to cross the lines of gender and organizational culture. But one definite key my friend zeroed in on was that I am willing to be myself.

For example, a male colleague once said, "It doesn't bother you at all that you're a female pastor, does it?" While I found the exact phrasing of his question a bit abrupt, I did understand what he was trying to say. He noticed that I don't defend myself publicly with those who oppose my right to this vocation. As such, my response to him that day remains the same as it would now.

I'm called. I know it. I am clear on what Jesus has done to redeem my life for this very thing, and I will not apologize for it. Some don't agree or approve, and that's beyond my control. But while I won't argue with them, I'm also not going to let them tell me I'm doing something wrong.

I was created a female, and I am also called by God. And since He has confirmed His call in my life as I search the Scriptures, there is nothing to be bothered about.

One of my favorite passages of Scripture is Psalm 139:13-16:

> *For you created my inmost being;*
> *you knit me together in my mother's womb.*
> *I praise you because I am fearfully and wonderfully made;*
> *your works are wonderful,*
> *I know that full well.*
> *My frame was not hidden from you*
> *when I was made in the secret place,*
> *when I was woven together in the depths of the earth.*
> *Your eyes saw my unformed body;*
> *all the days ordained for me were written in your book.*

Yes, God knew me before I came into existence. He created me and called me.

That's my certainty.

Whether you are male or female, I recommend that you personally study Scripture and draw your own conclusions about women in leadership – prayerfully and intellectually. Don't accept someone else's point of view without having studied the subject yourself. Increase your knowledge by reading other sources on the topic.[1]

Trust the Holy Spirit to reveal through Scripture what you can and cannot accept as correct instruction. And do not put down other people who don't agree with your point of view or let them condemn you if you don't see eye to eye.

The reality is that many Christians, both ministers and laypeople, have not reconciled how they think about clergywomen. Worse yet, they haven't come to terms with an understanding of what Scripture has to say on the subject.

For me, it's easier to respect a point of view that's been determined after a prayerful search of Scripture. It's hard to listen to someone who has an idea that something is wrong yet can't or won't articulate why.

In my opinion, Mark Twain had it completely right when he said, "It ain't what you know that gets you in trouble; it's what you know for sure that just ain't so."

Author Ruth Haley Barton, a former pastor, is now the founding president of The Transformation Center, a ministry dedicated to caring for the souls of pastors, ministry leaders, and the congregations and organizations they serve. She says:

> *I am not sure I changed my mind about women in leadership as much as I finally let myself believe something I had always known...* [2]
>
> *I learned that an examination of Scripture's themes reveals that "more than a hundred passages in the Bible affirm women in roles of leadership, and fewer than half a dozen appear to be in opposition," and I was shocked to realize that we as Christians had built an elaborate system of belief and practice on only a few difficult passages. These passages have loomed so large that we have allowed them to color everything else we read. We had lifted these passages out of their own context, out of the context of the broader themes of Scripture and elevated them to the point that they become more important than the overall message of Scripture on this topic.* [3]

Yet the idea is so foreign to some that they've never so much as thought of having a female pastor before. Either that or they aren't sure how to handle it.

In 2002, I conducted research for my master's thesis, surveying lay leaders who were in my geographic region from within my own denominational tribe. The questions I came up with were designed to help uncover if there was a difference in attitudes or beliefs about females having a *call to ministry* versus females holding the *position of pastor* according to the duties outlined in our denomination's manual. The result from one question was especially telling: Q7, which asked:

Which duties of the senior pastor listed in the survey do respondents perceive are more effectively carried out by a man versus a woman?

The duties listed were:

- To preach the word
- To equip the saints for the work of the ministry
- To administer the sacraments
- To care for the people by pastoral visitation, particularly the sick and needy
- To comfort those who mourn
- To correct, rebuke and encourage, with great patience and careful instruction
- To have the care of all departments of local church work

Certain trends clearly stood out. Respondents strongly favored men to effectively carry out the duties of:

- Preaching (91%)
- Equipping the saints for ministry (72%)
- Administration of the sacraments (84%)
- Correction and instruction of the congregation (76%)
- Overall care of all departments of the church (66%)

Whereas women were strongly favored to effectively carry out duties in:

- Pastoral visitation, particularly for the sick and needy (62%)
- Comforting those who mourn (68%)

But if those are the expectations, which seem to automatically accept the traditional roles Western woman have as the mothering type, they run the serious risk of playing out poorly for women who are strong pastoral leaders. They also do a disservice to men who have high gifts of mercy yet are automatically expected to be strong in correcting and rebuking.

Overall, I'm happy to say the majority of the survey's findings were more favorable than expected. Yet two telling responses served to underscore the mindsets shown above, stating what many people still believe even if they don't publicly express it.

God's ideal plan was for a male to be the spiritual leader of the family. Often females are because the man won't – 2nd best. A married pastor (female) creates problems in the family and church as to who is the spiritual leader in the family. This is a real problem today – who is in charge? What is headship, submission, etc.? Many marriages are in trouble because of this. A married female pastor only makes this problem worse. A single female pastor would not cause any problem in this area. Scripture is not clear on women in ministry, but it is clear on who the spiritual leader of the family is.

– Anonymous male respondent

I felt compelled to add some comments since your survey didn't allow for an in-between. For instance, I do not feel that the Bible specifically addresses senior pastors as being only a man's job. But I think it makes it clear in Ephesians that a wife is to submit to her husband as the husband submits to Christ. Therefore, I feel a married woman shouldn't serve as a senior pastor, but I think a single woman could serve as a senior pastor. Also, the term "pastor" in question 7 could mean "caretaker of the flock," and I think a woman could do that job better than a man if it means visiting the sick and making sure people are "connected." Also, I think a woman is called by God to teach a Bible study or Sunday School… or other women and children.

– Anonymous female respondent

Get the idea?

Views about what roles are and aren't Biblical or appropriate run deep. And it's important to note that these responses come from leaders in a denomination that has always – always! – ordained women. Yet I know of numerous situations where clergywomen were unable to get an interview with a church board because the people on them couldn't get past the traditional idea of having a male minister.

They couldn't imagine how it would be to have a female pastor.

It seems then that part of the change we need is one of mindset. And in my experience, actually having a clergywoman serve the church in either a paid or unpaid staff ministry role does that best. We need the opportunity to serve in our areas of calling. We need a place to prove ourselves, even though we wish it wasn't so. And we need allies to champion our voices, gifts and talents. Changing this mentality will take time, but it can be done. I know this for a fact.

When I first realized the call of God on my life to full-time pastoral ministry, I too wasn't sure if this was something He actually blessed. No one had ever discussed the topic around or with me. So I went to the best source I know: the Bible. I did a thorough study of Scripture, looking at passages used to validate the other point of view.

I read how "your sons and daughters will prophesy" in Joel 2:28 and again when it was quoted in Acts 2:17.

I intently examined how Jesus treated the women in his life.

I saw that Mary was the first one to see Jesus at the tomb and that she ran to tell others about it: an ambassador for the risen Lord.

Then there were the stories of Mary and Martha, Deborah, Esther, Ruth, the woman caught in adultery, and the Samaritan woman at the well, to name a few. I also studied texts written by scholars on the subject of women called to ministry, both pro and con. And I examined my heart in prayer, asking the Lord to give me wisdom "that I might not sin against Him."[4] This was my genuine and heartfelt prayer:

> *Search me, God, and know my heart;*
> *test me and know my anxious thoughts.*
> *See if there is any offensive way in me,*
> *and lead me in the everlasting way.*
>
> Psalm 139:23-24

After all of this, I felt more confirmation than ever that God was calling me and that Jesus himself would be kissing me on the cheek, giving me a hug and saying, "Shirley, I'll ride in the car with you. Start your engine and let's go!"

I'm working on my life story.
I'm not decided if it's going to be
a musical or a movie with music in it.

- Dolly Parton

CHAPTER 3

WHERE IT ALL STARTED

Before my calling, I never dreamed of being a pastor.

In fact, for a long time, I believed I might be one of the least likely people to have ever become one.

I grew up in the 1950s and '60s in southern New Jersey, the portion of the state that gave it "the Garden State" name. Especially back then, apple, peach and pear orchards produced delicious fruit all summer long. Fresh vegetables grew abundantly in multi-acre fields, and the vines and bushes were picked clean every harvest season by migrant workers who came to live in our community for just that purpose.

Today, most of those fields and orchards have been replaced by housing developments and shopping centers. But those fields were truly beautiful growing up.

Most everyone in my town knew everyone else – at least depending on the side of the tracks they lived on. Whites lived on one side of town; blacks in another. And although we went to school together, our neighborhoods were, for the most part, quite segregated -- especially on Sunday morning at church.

But time changes people and people change things. These days, individuals of all races and backgrounds live next to each other all across the town. Unfortunately though, not as much change has occurred on Sunday mornings. Church services continue to be quite segregated, something that is true in many communities.

As for my family, we were our own brand of different, forever impacted by what happened to Dad during World War II.

My father was drafted into the Army in the early 1940s, leaving behind his new bride and baby son, who was only nine months old. During a battle in the Philippines, a shell exploded near his foxhole, sending pieces of shrapnel flying. Fragments of metal hit him in the skull behind his right ear, slicing into his head. He was blinded instantly and lost hearing in his right ear as well.

After that, Dad came home a wounded veteran with several war medals, including a purple heart, but no way to earn a living. My parents did begin to receive veteran's pay and government benefits. They and their beautiful baby boy moved away to another state for many months while Dad received training on how to work with a Seeing Eye dog, how to read Braille, and how to raise chickens to help support our family.

When they returned home, their garage was converted into a chicken coop and my parents sold eggs and chickens for income. But they eventually had to stop earning money this way. As I'm told, rats got into the chicken feed. And since Dad couldn't see them, there was a high risk of him being bitten.

My father never physically saw his oldest son or wife again after military service. And he never saw his second son or me at all. Nor was that the only lasting effect of World War II he had to carry with him. The consequences of having shrapnel in his body – pieces the doctors of his day simply could not remove – would wage an internal war on his physical health in later years. He became very crippled, walking on crutches or with a walker, and eventually was confined to a wheelchair.

His being a blinded veteran with other disabilities shaped our whole world.

My mother was a homemaker, and she supported Dad through thick and thin. They were married for 51 years before he passed away and modeled for us what true commitment to marriage vows can look like.

Because of Dad's needs, Mom and I never did many of the "mother-daughter bonding" things that other women did. We didn't go on special shopping dates or travel together or spend one-on-one time outside of the house. It wasn't a bad life I led growing up, just different from the norms I saw with my friends.

Although I knew my parents loved me, I longed for more one-on-one attentiveness than my mother could give me. Without resentment, I understood that she had to focus on Dad. And I yearned to get big, strong hugs from Dad or sit on his lap for a story, two things he was physically unable to do. So to fulfill my emotional need for attention, I poured myself into activities where I could excel and receive praise or compliments, and into friendships with other kids that made me feel needed and noticed.

As a child, I was a straight-A student and my life was steeped in musical pursuits. I played piano from age six and then started violin lessons in third grade. While I was an extrovert who found social relationships through my many friends at church, school and other places, my life mainly revolved around school and orchestra practice.

By the age of 13, I was giving beginner lessons to violin students over the summer as well as beginner piano lessons. By my freshman year of high school, I played violin in several school orchestras, chamber music ensembles, and in both county and regional high school level orchestras. I also accompanied the school choir on piano and played dinner music at a local restaurant for the Lions Club.

My goal was to become an orchestra conductor. I wanted to play an instrument in every group – strings, brass, woodwinds and percussion – and I wanted to do this before I graduated high school. Thus, I added lessons on both the viola and saxophone in addition to piano and violin.

But I would never graduate from high school. At least not in the traditional sense.

A big part of my non-musical social life happened at the local roller-skating rink. My brother Marvin, the middle child, and I loved to skate. We would go to the rink at least four times a week, mingling with many of our school friends who were there as well.

But there was also another crowd who frequented the rink: people from other towns who we would have otherwise never encountered. People like the young man who would become my first husband.

From a nearby town, he was three years older than me. One evening, he asked me to skate with him and then began to regularly pay attention to me in a way that fed my need to be noticed. I had very low self-esteem at that time, some from normal teenaged insecurities and some as a result of being teased for being overweight. I also felt like I was different from other kids because our family life wasn't like everyone else's. In short, I had a lot of unmet emotional needs that impacted my behavior.

Even though I'd been taught better, I began to make poor choices in this new relationship because I craved the attention and typically tried to please people to gain acceptance. So I caved in to the pressure to have sex ("If you love me, you'll let me.") and, as a result, found myself pregnant at the end of my freshman year of high school.

I was only 15 years old.

I vividly remember the morning I confessed to my mother than I wasn't sure if I was pregnant or not. In that instant, everything changed in our home. My parents, needless to say, were devastated. For them, it was like an early death of their "good little girl" daughter and all their hopes and dreams for my future. I didn't realize until many years later that it was also humiliating for them to tell their friends. Socially, it reflected back on their parenting abilities.

My oldest brother was already married and living elsewhere with his new wife and baby, so the circumstances had little effect on them. However, my brother Marvin, who I was very close with, was in San Diego at the time, serving in the Navy. He, like my parents, was shocked when he got the news. He wrote me a long letter telling me how upset he was, but also how much he loved me and always would. My tender ego needed to hear that so badly.

That was 1967... and I still have that letter.

At school, I had to face my teachers and get their signatures verifying that all my books had been turned in for the year since I would not be back in the fall. In those days, girls did not go back to school when they were "in the family way." They didn't really go back anywhere. My mother had to petition the court and get a judge's signature to allow me to marry because I was underage.

I still remember the day we went to court. It must have been so awful for her.

In my social circles, I was labeled by many as a slut or worse, and ostracized by the community of people I had always known. Other kids didn't talk to me anymore, though I realize now that a lot of people just didn't know what to say. In their eyes, I was one of the girls least likely to get pregnant. (There's that "least likely" thing again!)

Tragically, another girl from school got pregnant at the same time I did, and her family was so humiliated that they sold their business and moved far away to Florida. That's how differently teen pregnancy was viewed then. It was like wearing a scarlet letter.

So in July of 1967, I married the father of my child; and the very next January, 12 days after my 16th birthday, I gave birth to a healthy, beautiful baby boy. By the time I was 20, I had another son and a baby girl.

And my husband had become a full-blown alcoholic.

Because I was young and naïve, I didn't realize he had a problem with alcohol even before we got married, despite the reality that the signs were there. But I definitely got the message after the fact, complete with five long years of physical, mental, verbal and emotional abuse.

My parents went through hell watching the mess of my married life and its final demise. My husband's abuse toward the children and me manifested itself on many levels, and his constant marital unfaithfulness only added to the misery. Alcohol had replaced me as my husband's first love. Drinking brought out the worst in him, grossly distorting any possibility we had of having a happy, peaceful home.

I left my husband when I was 20, with three children under the age of five, one of whom was a three-month-old baby. I had no high school diploma and no way to support myself beyond the low-paying jobs I managed to get. To make ends meet, I had to live on welfare, food stamps and Medicaid insurance for eight years.

During that time, I studied hard to get my General Education Diploma, or GED, for high school. Then I went on to college for an Associates degree in retail management, all while working full-time as a store clerk and holding other entry-level jobs. It wasn't easy, to say the least, but I thank God for my parents, who helped as much as they could.

One of the jobs I had was as a waitress at a local diner, where I often worked past midnight. Because my babysitter often spent the night, I would go out after work with another waitress to let off steam at a nearby nightclub. For a few short hours, I would try to escape facing reality by dancing and drinking alcohol – the very drug that messed up my marriage in the first place. How incredibly stupid!

It's amazing what we will do to bury our pain. I only wish I had known the love of Jesus then and the beautiful alternative of coping with life in Christ.

One night, my waitress friend ran into a guy named Ron who she knew from high school; and she introduced us at the bar. Like me, Ron was separated and getting a divorce, and we struck up a friendship. We eventually dated and became lovers, and then he moved in with the kids and me. We lived together for six years and, during that time, he helped by working full time, then coming home to watch the kids and do various household chores while I finished homework for school.

I don't think I would have graduated had I not had his support along with my parents'.

Even though I had been raised in church, I certainly did not have a relationship with Christ during that time, let alone any plan to become a minister. Ron had also grown up going to church with his parents, but neither of us ever understood nor experienced a saving relationship with Christ. We were just living life, trying to get by.

His stepfather and mother were both devout Christians, and they nagged us all the time about getting the kids and ourselves into church. We finally tried going to a few places just to get them off our backs, but we were living together unmarried, which was viewed very differently in the '70s than today. So as soon as we began to explain our different last names, the looks we got said it all. No one had to say it out loud. Their communication through body language and physical withdraw from us let us know very clearly...

You're not welcome here.

Don't bring your trashy lifestyle into our church. You might contaminate our kids.

This response was especially taxing on me. While I had been out of church for a long time by then, I could still remember what it had been like to be part of that kind of community.

You see, I had been an active part of the youth group right up until I got pregnant. Yet no one from church ever contacted me after that. Nonetheless, soon after giving birth to my first child, I felt drawn to go back and so I attended a service. Sitting in the pew behind me was a woman who had been my Sunday School teacher when I was in elementary school. She didn't speak *to* me that day, but she did speak *about* me.

I heard her whispering with a tone of disgust to the person next to her, "She's the one: the one who got pregnant and had a baby."

I was crushed.

After that, I stayed out of church for over 10 years. I often wonder how different my life might have been if she had shown compassion and love to me that day.

I'll never know, of course. But it did motivate me to be sure I don't do the same to someone else. Compassion always wins over judgment. It doesn't mean we have to agree with a person's behavior, but we can extend mercy and forgiveness just like Jesus did. After all, the Bible says we've all sinned – we all fall short of what God desires from us – yet God offers us His free gift of salvation by grace through faith in Jesus Christ. And God has a way of taking care of things and setting people straight without our interference.

I believe in prevenient grace: the grace that goes before us. God is always watching, and He knows us while we're still steeped in our sin. While one person or even many people may condemn us, He can use others to intervene and speak truth into our lives – truth that helps us find the right path.

One such person the Lord used in Ron's and my life was a school counselor from our son's elementary school. In 1978, he approached us to bravely and compassionately confront us with the fact that our lack of relational commitment to each other – that is, choosing to live together without being married – was affecting our oldest child emotionally.

As the eldest, he had been most affected by the loss and grief caused by my divorce from his biological father. Now he was showing signs of feeling vulnerable and insecure because, as a child, he couldn't figure out whether Ron and I would stay together. If divorce happened once, he reasoned, another separation could happen again at any time. And this reality was affecting his sense of well-being on a deep level.

Recognizing the truth of what the counselor told us, Ron and I decided to stop just living together and get married. Our wedding took place in March of 1979, and we began attending church shortly thereafter thanks to Ron's brother. He had accepted Jesus as his Savior and was being baptized by full immersion, something we had never witnessed before. So, at his invitation, we went to see him get dunked.

There, we heard the testimonies of people who professed that Jesus had changed their lives. We watched as they went down in the water and came up wiping their smiling faces while a big group of people from the church clapped and cheered in celebration with them.

The people in attendance treated us so warmly. They welcomed us and showed genuine interest in who we were and how we were.

This was early summer.

Only two months later, as the pastor spoke from God's word at an evening service, both Ron and I individually found our heads and our hearts immersed in the sermon. The result was that we each recognized our need for God. In response, we both left our seats to go to the front of the sanctuary to kneel at the altar to pray. Ron went out one side of the row, and I went out the other. We were both so caught up in the gospel message that neither of us realized the other had come forward until after the service.

The pastor, Rev. Stephen Grosvenor, and people of this local church shared with us the way of salvation: of how to confess our sins and ask Christ to come into our lives. We both did – and our lives were never the same again. After that, knowing Christ created the foundation for our marriage through years that were both thick and thin.

We've been a couple for 46 years now and counting. All glory to God!

Within a few months of that altar call, we celebrated another baptism service, this one in my mom and dad's swimming pool. We were now the new believers being immersed, testifying to how Christ had saved us from our sins.

Within the next few years, my parents would join us in a Bible study and eventually rededicate their lives to Christ as well. I found out that they had known Christ years before, and although morally good people, they had stopped focusing much on their Christian faith. But after this, they both attended church regularly and served the Lord with great zeal until the day they died.

This is the past I came from. This is the journey I made. And that is the story of what God did with my life – at least the first part.

And as for my earlier statement about being a pastor, that "I might be one of the least likely people to have ever become one," well, I know better now. There is nothing in Scripture to support the idea that a certain kind of person with a certain kind of background can't be called to lead in the Kingdom of God.

A colleague and good friend of mine, Rev. Byron Hannon, recently reminded me of this when he wrote me how: "It's ironic that we so easily assume that our broken past disqualifies us from the leadership over GOD's people. Moses was a runaway murderer, stuck on the backside of the desert, shepherding his father-in-law's sheep. Many of the first disciples were anything but acceptable; just poor, unlearned men and the simple women in their circle who were of no account."

So for any of us to make the claim that we are the "least likely" to be a pastor or serve in church leadership immediately identifies us as exactly the kind of person the Lord called on regularly. The Kingdom of God does not work the same way as the world around us. The "top down" perspective of leadership and hierarchical power that's been modeled for us in organizational systems was an issue that Jesus repeatedly addressed with the Pharisees.

This was the kind of leader they expected their Messiah to be: the kind of legislative structure they expected him to create as he fulfilled the Law they knew so well. But Jesus went so far as to tell them in Matthew 20:28, "...the Son of Man [Jesus] did not come to be served, but to serve, and to give his life as a ransom for many."

Not exactly a "top down" declaration.

Instead, Jesus ministered to and from the opposite direction – from the bottom up – as he was deeply concerned with those at the lowermost end of the socioeconomic rungs. That's where I was when I encountered a life-changing relationship with Him.

Perhaps someone who is reading this will identify with the mistakes I've made in my past. Yours may be different than mine, yet they have shaped you into who you are today. Maybe others have never experienced things like this in life. You have known Christ since childhood and always been faithful and true to the Lord.

Either way, I praise God for your testimony. People need to know that Christ can bring us out of our troubles and into a better place. They also need to know that Christ can keep us from going there at all.

No matter our background, it's wonderful to know that we are worthy simply by virtue of His love for us. And if the Lord has placed a call on our lives to serve like he served, we can do so knowing that we are precisely the kind of person God has chosen to spread His love!

Thanks be to God!

CHAPTER 4

CHANGING LANES

God makes clear where our journey in life is headed, even when we don't expect it. And we can believe and act on God's will when it becomes blatantly evident.

That's faith.

I recently attended a pastor's training seminar where the guest speaker told of all the people in his family who had come before him in pastoral ministry. He told of his father, grandfather and uncles. And now his children were following in his footsteps too. It was a beautiful story.

I admit that it always stirs me deep within to hear individuals, especially those in pastoral ministry, chronicle such a rich heritage of Christian family. What a foundation.

As a new member of the clergy, I often asked God, "Why me?" After all, there are no pastors in the family line before me that I know of. Nor are there any pastors coming behind me in the family line that I know of.

The answer the Lord always impressed upon me is this: *Why not you?*

My journey to ordained ministry started in 1994. As I mentioned earlier, I had worked hard to establish a career in sales and marketing before that, and it was flourishing at the time. As the founder and owner of a national telesales consultancy, I was a published author in my field, a frequent speaker at conferences across the country, and earning a really good living. All the dreams and wishes I'd had for my entrepreneurial career were coming to fruition. The sacrifice of time away from family and the many other personal costs of owning a business all seemed worth it. I was content in so many ways.

But then God began to do a new work in me.

It started out with what felt like a confusing change in perspective. Work that had always energized me started becoming something I dreaded. I'd go into a company to consult or conduct several days of training in sales or customer service skills, and it just didn't feel right anymore.

I found myself noticing details about the people I met. They would have salaries well exceeding mine, yet they were discontent. Their income would never be enough, leaving them depressed and sad.

I was seeing how people felt locked into corners they couldn't get out of. Some couldn't risk giving up their jobs because they could never top the compensation and benefits. Others couldn't leave because they didn't think they could get another job at all. And above and beyond that, so many of the people I met needed hope, encouragement or contentment regarding the things they were facing in life.

They needed what I was finding in Jesus.

I recognized this on such a deep level that my soul ached for them. When I'd come home, I would tell Ron, "I wish I was telling them about Jesus." And I meant it.

Clearly, something was stirring within me. My call was taking shape. And I am so fortunate to have received that call while under the leadership of a minister who clearly understood what was happening to me. I certainly didn't know! Yet my pastor, Dr. Chuck Gates, listened as I processed my life out loud over and over again until he finally sat me down for a serious talk.

"Shirley, I believe you're experiencing a classic call to full-time ministry," he told me.

"What's that?" I asked, with no idea what he was talking about. What more could there possibly be to my Christian calling than what I was already doing?

Ever since accepting Christ into my life in 1979, I'd been a very active layperson. I taught Sunday school, played piano for worship, helped with church marketing plans, sang in the choir… You name it, I did it. I was already giving so much time and energy to the church, and I loved every minute of it.

What more was there for me to do?

Pastor Gates went on to precisely answer that question. "What you're describing sounds like God is talking with you about giving your whole self as a minister. A 'call' goes beyond being an active layperson. It means your entire life is given to ministry for the people of God. It's a pastoral calling for life."

This pastor, good friend and to-be mentor of mine was the first person to identify my call to ministry. I am forever grateful that he had the spiritual discernment and courage to talk to me about it.

There's a lesson here for male and female clergy alike. We're responsible to watch for others among us who may be experiencing that kind of leading into full-time service. I genuinely don't know where I would be today if my pastor hadn't seen what God was doing in me. This can be true for both genders, but perhaps especially for young girls and women who may never meet a clergywoman and therefore not realize the options before them: how they too can preach sermons, pastor churches, be chaplains or otherwise lead God's people as ordained elders.

I took Pastor Gates' words home and talked with Ron, who confirmed my own thinking that this seemed like a genuine possibility. He went even further in recommending that I find someone to talk to who had nothing to gain from how I responded. You see, Pastor Gates had suggested I come work in the church to further explore my calling, and Ron wanted to make sure my motivation was unbridled in the decision process.

That's how I found myself visiting a retired elder for whom I had great respect. He and his wife met with me – there's that not being alone with a woman thing again – and I told him my story: how I was struggling with my business perspective, what I was feeling when I came home, and what my pastor had said to me about a call.

After listening intently, this gentleman agreed that God was awakening something new within me. And then he took it one step further by asking a critical question. It's the question God used to confirm His will in my life.

"Are you aware that our denomination just began offering a ministry track to prepare for ordination as a of deacon of administration? Perhaps this is a place for you to start."

Sitting there, he had no idea that administration is one of my highest spiritual gifts. It's something I enjoy so much and that God has used to help others in so many ways. So, just like that, I found the confirmation I needed.

God was speaking. I was listening. And the course of my life would never be the same.

When I went home and told Ron everything, he also received it as confirmation. As the most important person in my life, his support of my call from the very beginning was instrumental in helping me follow God's lead. I didn't believe that a loving God would call me to something that would cause conflict in our otherwise healthy Christian marriage, especially when we both knew that, if I followed this path, it would impact the way we lived.

This included financially.

Up until then, Ron and I had always shared the responsibility for bringing income into our home. Sometimes he made more money than me; occasionally I made more money than him. But unlike with some couples, our relationship was unfazed by those fluctuations. Thankfully, Ron is very secure in who he is in Christ, and our marriage is built on that same kind of certainty. So that's how we entered into this new calling as well.

I said "yes" to God's call and the church. My pastoral journey had begun, with plenty of adventures on the road ahead!

There wasn't anything rushed about the process. It was about three years from the time this all started before I took my first pastoral job. By that point, I'd had a lot of time to think over many of the potential aspects of living a pastor's life. Yet that didn't mean there weren't significant mental, psychological, emotional and, yes, financial adjustments still to be made.

As the time came for each of these adjustments, I processed them, argued with God, vacillated, listened some more, and finally understood what I had to do. I began by closing down my business, and we sold our dream farmhouse on its eight wonderful acres to move to a smaller, more affordable home.

The recently purchased new car had to go too. Accepting that first official assignment at the church meant that my income was reduced to one-third of what I had been making. And there were no benefits involved or tax write-offs for travel.

Nothing.

Our kids thought I was crazy and, admittedly, the risks did seem high as I stepped out in faith to take my first pastoral position as an administrative pastor at my home church. But this one thing I knew for sure – God was calling me. And if I didn't answer yes, I could no longer honestly say I was following Him completely.

Due to family and financial constraints, I didn't study for ordination by attending seminary like most pastors do. Instead, I completed the educational requirements through classes offered by my district and region.

> Progress always involves risk; you can't steal second base and keep your foot on first.
> *Frederick Wilcox*

I was 47 years old when I was ordained as an elder, and I was 48 years old when I was finally able to finish my Bachelor of Arts in Organizational Management. (I'm only telling you my age here to encourage those women who might think it's too late for them to complete their education and the work required for ordination. It's not!) I then earned my Masters Degree in Organizational Leadership at the age of 51 through a collaborative program between Eastern University in St. Davids, Pennsylvania, and Cornerstone Christian College in Cape Town, South Africa.

I was the only American student involved in that latter cohort and was able to take two trips to Cape Town before receiving my degree, adding richness to my cross-cultural experiences.

And I will say this: Although my particular circumstances during that season drove most of my decisions about how to finish my education, one of my regrets to this day is not having a seminary experience. I've found it challenging as a pastor, and still do, to round out my theological perspectives. I've always had to study extra hard to make sure I present the Scriptures as accurately as possible. I believe if I'd gotten a seminary education, such things would have come more naturally.

It's like how you don't know what you don't know – you know?

I was always aware that not completing high school in the traditional sense had left me with certain information gaps. It's been the same with my theological education. But I am so blessed and grateful that various teachers, friends and spiritual mentors have supplemented my reading and studying along the way.

They've answered so many of my questions, helping me fill in those educational gaps through dialogue and debate. Their insights, answers and feedback have pointed me toward a healthier and more informed understanding and application of the specific theological perspectives that I hold. And they've also been amazingly instrumental in shaping me to become a good preacher. Them and God's guidance, of course. I can't tell you how much I've leaned on the Holy Spirit to guide and direct me all along the way. And I still do.

Over the years, I have often been asked how I learned to preach. I admit that having a public speaking background was very helpful; and being a natural extrovert, I'm not afraid to be up in front of people. Give me a microphone, and I can find something to say.

Yet preaching my first sermon was still quite memorable for me.

I cannot tell you what the passage was. But I can vividly recall thinking about how I was going to stand up and speak on God's behalf. What a profound moment that was! There was a sense of responsibility like I'd never felt before – one I still feel even after all these years. It is a privilege and a sacred honor to bring the Word of God to the people of God, and it should never be treated as less.

I try to employ the best of my skills and talents to this end. Again, that means accepting and even seeking constructive feedback as I go along. For example, one helpful piece of advice came early on from my evangelist friend, Dr. Stephen Manley. Stephen has a unique delivery style and can preach many messages from the same passage. I've listened to him give numerous sermons using the exact same Scripture reference, but each one had a unique and defined main point. He is a master at this style of preaching and refers to his study technique as "saturation".

When Stephen first introduced me to the concept of saturation, I began to apply it to my own Bible reading and study time. Simply put, it's a charge to slow down and stop reading when a passage of Scripture hits you – when it seems to be saying something important, stirring something inside you that needs more thought or consideration.

When that happens, stay there. Don't rush on. Just sit with the passage, pray over it, and wait until the essence of it is dripping out of you... like picking up and squeezing a sponge that's been soaking in water. This model really worked for me.

Stephen was also exceptionally instrumental in allowing me to see myself realistically as I learned the ropes. And when, during my first pastorate, I asked him some questions about preaching methods, he suggested that it would likely take me a year or so to get a feel for my personal style in the pulpit.

He was right on that one too.

Over the years, my preaching evolved into a style that is primarily expository. I love to take words apart and play with concepts. But even more than that, I love to look at Bible characters and see how we might feel or how we would experience the story if we were in their shoes. Through that perspective, I hope to bring listeners into their own encounters with Jesus.

Another great influence was John MacArthur's' *Ashamed of the Gospel*, one of the books I read early on in my calling. It purports that there is nothing much else to talk about from the pulpit but Jesus. Jesus is the number one character – the living, giving, life-changing person.

That struck me as good advice. So I prepare sermons always remembering that Jesus is the main character of the salvation story. He is the focal point. And, as much as possible, I look for and use supportive illustrations for my sermon points that can be gleaned from other Scripture stories rather than the news, internet or pop culture. That's a lot easier than you might think when the Bible is such a rich resource!

I also try to avoid talking about myself too much from the pulpit, using personal illustrations only when they are the absolute best way to make my point or will help listeners connect with me. And I never, ever use illustrations from our family life without permission.

Another helpful technique I've used to think about the result of any one sermon is the three-point method of asking: What does it say? What does it mean? How does it apply? I believe it's my responsibility to bring the passage to life and help people understand what the text is saying and what it means in the broader context of Scripture.

Despite all of that careful thought and consideration, most pastors I know have at least a sermon or two we wish we could preach over again – for the sole reason that we don't feel they were good enough the first time around. Perhaps they weren't fully developed enough to be ready just yet. Maybe we feel like we missed the point.

Yet sometimes when we think we failed to communicate well, it's only to find that the Holy Spirit is working and moving among the people in ways we could not have anticipated. And we get to see the results of God's Word working in people's lives. Thus, I quickly learned to trust the Spirit for results, focusing instead on the craft of delivery.

To this end, I have always kept the practice of listening to my sermons after giving them in order to evaluate my presentation style. There are certain words I use that can become repetitive, and perhaps, even annoying to listeners.

Right?

(That's one of them, by the way.)

The voice is an amazing communication tool. But I've been surprised over the years with how resistant some pastors are to hearing themselves preach. While I was in business, I attended professional training on presentation skills. There, everyone in the class was videotaped and had to listen *and* watch themselves talk. I admit it was awkward at first to observe myself this way. But it definitely helped me see how I came across in a real-time audiovisual format.

It unquestionably helped me become more effective as a communicator. This training method helps maximize the total package of skills needed to present a message using both voice and body language. And when applied to the context of preaching, all pastors want to do their best to present the gospel in a way that holds people's interest, gains attention and gets a response from the listeners.

If I'm listening to myself in an audio-only format, I reflect on how my voice inflection, tone or volume impacts the delivery to make it better or worse. This is the same set of skills I used to teach representatives who worked in telesales and customer service centers. Your voice is all you have in those contexts – and you never get a second chance to make a first impression.

Thus, I consider techniques like:

- Speeding up or slowing down appropriately (People in the Northeast tend to talk fast, yet most people can listen faster than a person can talk)
- Being loud and/or quiet to create emphasis
- Using pregnant pauses for effect
- Hearing my pitch (I get high-pitched when I'm excited or going too fast)
- Analyzing whether I sounded excited about it or if I came across as bored or boring

While I can't go back and preach that sermon again, I can find patterns to reinforce what worked well and better avoid aspects that did not. I can also listen again to the structure of the sermon. For example: Did my illustrations work well? Was I story telling or just spitting out facts? Since I have an expository style, I have to work purposefully to avoid just citing the facts of a text, instead packing them into a narrative story to relay the message.

I'm not suggesting that this type of evaluation should be done on every sermon. But at least from time to time, a speaker can listen or watch to improve their skills. As I mentioned before, not everyone wants to do this type of self-assessment. However, if my former church had a video recorder along with its audio capabilities, I would have also utilized that once in a while for just this purpose.

It's simply one more way to perfect the craft of speaking to people, and I highly recommend it to all those I mentor. The idea is to evaluate your skills, not to be overly critical or self-deprecating. There are far too many other opportunities to fall into that trap anyway.

Lastly, I always have the specific congregation or audience in mind when I prepare a sermon. Whether I'm preaching on a regular basis to the same congregation or speaking at churches where I don't know a soul, I know that there are people filtering what I say through a variety of personality temperaments and with differing life experiences and circumstances. Each will hear and respond uniquely.

While I can offer relevant illustrations of how my subject matter can apply to life, I totally understand that the final application is determined solely by each person's response to what the Holy Spirit says from the message. I am not responsible for this, and it's fruitless to think that everyone will get the same exact point.

They often don't even get the overarching point I was trying to make! I've had people talk to me about sermons I've preached where I don't even recognize what they're saying because it wasn't even close what I intended. Yet they still received a worthwhile message.

This is the movement of the Holy Spirit! God's word will speak one way or another. That is a direct and verifiable promise from the Lord.

Preaching is such a privilege and the most exciting, fulfilling thing I have ever done as a pastor. And even though I once never dreamt of being a clergywoman, I now can't imagine my life now if I hadn't said yes to God. There are no regrets – not one. It has been a joy to serve the Lord and His church in this way, even with the ups and downs that come along with the vocation.

I've learned that, when we follow God's plan and know we're doing what he wants, regardless of our vocation, it's the greatest feeling of contentment in the world.

Pastor and author Eugene H. Peterson once said, "I believe God takes the things in our lives – family, background, education – and uses them as part of His calling. It might not be to become a pastor. But I don't think God wastes anything."

I say amen to that.

And maybe, just maybe, there will someday be someone in my family who stands before others and tells the story of how a woman in their family line was a pastor before them. You just never know who might be next!

CHAPTER 5

DON'T RIDE ALONE

Pastor.

My new identity.

My first ministry assignment was in my home church among people who had known me as just "Shirley" for over 15 years. So it sounded very odd to hear them begin to address me as "Pastor Shirley." The addition of "pastor" to my name took some time to get used to before it became normal for them or me to hear.

Moreover, not everyone opted to use this new title, and that was fine with me. It was my pastor who requested that the church openly acknowledge my calling and position; and, over time, more and more people did begin to call me "pastor". But it took a while, since the majority had known me for so long before all this happened.

As I started this new role with no experience or family predecessors to turn to for advice, I wondered how I would ever learn all the duties and responsibilities this vocation involved.

Like most new ministers, I needed to acquire the practical skills for pastoral ministry. But I also wanted to learn how to *be* a pastor and minister effectively with God's people.

Dr. Lovett Weems, distinguished professor of church leadership at Wesley Theological Seminary, describes the mentoring process for clergy as: "the journey from readiness for ministry to effectiveness for ministry." [1] That was exactly where I was at the time – ready, but not sure how to be effective. I needed help for sure!

So I began to look to other pastors who served near me, observing in them the things I wanted to know. I tried to identify people I could imitate as I looked for ways to learn and grow in my own role. Positive role models; energetic champions; and trustworthy, capable mentors were exactly what I needed for this ride.

In the beginning, my ministry models were almost exclusively men. Because I had worked with so many male leaders in business, this felt familiar and was of little concern to me. However, I would soon discover that there were distinct differences between business and ministry, yet another aspect of that culture shock we discussed before.

While I was interested in how these individuals did their pastoral work, I was even more intrigued to observe how they handled themselves in the process.

The pastors I knew back then – those I've stayed close to and those I still meet today – all have different styles of leadership and operate in a unique context within their local church or ministry. So I've watched men lead, and I've watched men fail to lead. I've also learned from both, seeing up close how issues of integrity – both personal and professional – are so important in ministry.

I know men who have guided their churches with tenacity and honor through very good and very difficult times alike. I've seen men who, like me, had awful, untrue things said about them: accusations that challenged their character as leaders with no appropriate way to publicly respond. I've been in the room as grown men cried over the pain and hurt of ministry, just like women can do. And I've been privileged to see them turn to the Lord for help, dig into Scripture, pray and hold their heads high even when they didn't feel like it.

What great models!

In more recent years, I'm happy to say I've also found many females in ministry to look up to. One of my closest female friends, the woman I referred in chapter one who I traveled the country with, is someone I first met in the ladies' room at church years before I became a pastor.

I was a baby Christian at the time and she wasn't a Christian at all, having only been invited to church by her brother. Stopping at the restroom before she left, Dawn and I ran into each other and ended up chatting for a few minutes, where we found out we had a lot in common as business professionals. It sparked a friendship and she kept coming to church, eventually giving her heart and life to the Lord.

Several years later, the same pastor who recognized the call on my life spoke to Dawn about how he saw God moving the same way in hers. And while, at first, she strongly resisted the idea, it was not long after that conversation when we were all together listening to Dr. Nina Gunter preach during a missions service. At the end of her message, she invited those who felt called to ministry to respond, and we sat awestruck as Dawn stepped out in faith that night to accept God's call on her life.

Pastor Dawn was single when she became a clergywoman. A gifted and talented woman who's overcome many obstacles in life, she's now bi-vocational, serving as the lead pastor of a church, and also working several days a week as a group facilitator in a women's correctional facility and a prevention specialist for at-risk juveniles. Pastor Dawn has invested her life into giving back; and in so doing, she's helped many individuals who are down and out.

Through her example, this friend of mine has repeatedly modeled what it means to be a woman of integrity – no matter what situations are thrown her way, bad or good. She's attractive and has had men in the church approach her with inappropriate advances more than once. She's encountered former addicts with mental health issues who have threatened her life. And she lived alone for a long time, yet still handled the day-to-day pressures of life and ministry with tenacity, grace, and compassion.

A few years ago, the Lord unexpectedly brought a wonderful man named Wil into her life. He was also a pastor at the time in Cape Town, South Africa. They are now married and serve in the U.S. together as bi-vocational pastors.

Pastor Dawn is a regular blessing to those who get to know her. And her enthusiasm for God is downright contagious. Ministry has definitely presented challenging moments for her, yet she remains both a model and one of my heroes of the faith.

I've also been privileged to work with women like Dr. Tammy Carter, who heads the initiative for the Wesleyan Holiness Digital Library,[2] working behind the scenes most of the time in this capacity. She is also the pastor of a church in an urban setting where people's needs are great. You can hear the love in her voice when she talks about her people! Her kind, sweet spirit leans into their lives to share the pain and allow them to find help and hope.

Tammy is the mother of two children, one of whom faced physical health challenges for many years. She has also been a caregiver for her aging mother at times. I've watched her juggle all these responsibilities while she simultaneously traveled the world representing her denomination and the digital library so that ministers and students from other countries and language groups could have access to the best tools and resources for spiritual growth and church health.

That's a lot!

Yet despite that busy schedule and all of her commitments, Tammy always greets me with a smile and asks how I'm doing. Her passion for what she's doing simply bubbles out of her. After just a brief conversation, you can tell that she is zealous about the value of this work.

Tammy exemplifies for me what it means to be sold out to the Lord and His calling. She remains dedicated and happy about what she's called to do, even when there are difficult or challenging moments in life.

What a great model!

Because of her, Pastor Dawn and many other exceptional clergywomen, I've always been especially sensitive to the model I myself am to young women who may be called to ministry or leadership positions in the future. Some of the young girls in the churches I've served in have always known a woman pastor. They watch how I preach, teach, lead, act, dress and handle myself with people. And through all that, they're learning that they can be called to preach or pastor too. That's a healthy perspective to offer them.

Of course, not everyone agrees with that last statement. So we'll address it in more detail later on. For now, let's just consider a quote from pastor, sociologist, author and public speaker Dr. Tony Campolo, who aptly states:

> Denying women the right to preach affects more than just those who are gifted and called to do so. This denial sends a message to all women – and especially young girls who are trying to figure out who they are – that they are inferior to men. Oh, those Christian leaders who say otherwise will make their case by stating that just because women have different callings from those of men, that does not make them inferior. But I argue that when they tell women that they are barred from the high calling of God to preach because they *are* women, these leaders have made a sexist statement that drowns out any verbal theological tap dancing they may do when they make their assertions.[3]

That "tap dancing" can be a learned behavior from never actually seeing women preach. But it doesn't have to be. A clergywoman friend once told the story of going on vacation and taking her children to another church to visit. Upon entering the sanctuary and seeing a male minister at the pulpit, her little boy exclaimed, "Mommy! Can men preach too?" He had always had a female pastor, so he had a revelation that day! He didn't know that having a male preacher was an option.

Isn't it great that we can teach our boys and girls to respect the gifts and callings that enable both genders to glorify God this way?

In addition to positive role models, clergywomen also benefit from having champions in their lives. These are people who go above and beyond to support the honor and call of female clergy, helping women achieve their highest potential in ministry.

Some of my personal champions include men in other leadership positions who have suggested my name for national committees, teams and speaking engagements that no one would have considered me for otherwise... men who have *publicly* affirmed and encouraged me as a pastor... men who recognize that the brotherhood is enriched when it includes the sisterhood... men who are intentional about including women in leadership, who are careful to use gender-inclusive language and who correct others who do not.

These men and I have strategized together, and they have accepted my ideas and input as valuable contributions to the discussion. They listen, and they hear.

I'm especially thankful for the example they set for other men, even those who don't yet share their beliefs on women in ministry. They advocate for us in places where we cannot advocate for ourselves. These champions understand how important their role is in making a way for women to access places and positions that aren't always open possibilities for my gender.

In my interactions with them, I greatly appreciate their purposeful language and the fact that they've neither placated nor advanced me based on my gender alone. Instead, they encourage me based on who I am and the call God has placed in my life. This is a standard they apply across the board, as I've seen them intentionally pay the same kind of positive attention to other capable women in ministry.

They're consistent.

I am so grateful for men like this, especially when I know that not all clergywomen find these champions. Fortunately, women who have already found a place in leadership as pastors, professors and administrative professionals are also recognizing the need to seize this same initiative. They are helping to pave the way for other capable women to step into their distinctive roles as well.

Dr. Carla Sunberg is one shining example of this for me. Currently the only female general superintendent for the Church of the Nazarene, she has championed the cause of women for many years. From her own life's experiences as a pastor's kid, a nurse, a missionary, a pastor, a district superintendent and a seminary president – and now in her current role – Carla has been a vocal advocate for clergywomen in her denomination. She understands firsthand the challenges and obstacles we face and has found creative and productive ways to address them to people in authority who can influence further change.

Another female champion is Dr. Nina Gunter, who preached in a stadium with over 20,000 people in attendance the night that Pastor Dawn was called. Nina was the first female general superintendent in the Nazarene denomination, and her forthright manner is embodied in love.

Having been called to ministry as a young girl, she is a proficient preacher, not to mention masterful at greeting people by their first names. I really don't know how she remembers so many, but she does. This alone makes people feel special around her, particularly when her service to the church is marked with such stamina, determination, passion and excellence. I have learned a lot by watching her professional demeanor, her enthusiasm for God and His Word, and her impeccable way of dressing in vibrant colors that celebrate her personality. She models what it means to be comfortable in your own skin.

I also had the privilege while in Philadelphia to work side by side with a dynamic clergywoman name Rev. Bonnie Camarda. Born in Cuba and raised in Spain, Bonnie is one of the most positive, energetic clergywomen I know. She has served as the Director of Church Partnerships and a Program Development Specialist with the Salvation Army in Philadelphia since 1999.

Her accomplishments are many and well known throughout the city of Philadelphia and beyond. Bonnie served as a board member for many organizations, including the Philadelphia Leadership Foundation and Esperanza Health Services. And at the time we worked together, Bonnie led weekly prayer meetings in the mayor's office, and interacted with both state and national governmental and religious leaders. Today she remains a clergywoman of presence in the city, region, nation and world.

I like to say that there isn't a person Bonnie hasn't met! We collaborated on various projects and, whenever I saw Bonnie at an event, the first thing she would ask is, "Have you met so-and-so?" Then she would take my hand and across the room we'd go to make introductions, shake hands and fill in gaps about why so-and-so and I should connect. She is one of the best networkers I've ever met, and her desire to connect people obviously brings her joy.

Bonnie not only offered me her friendship and support: she was one of my champions. She connected me with the Philadelphia Leadership Foundation and introduced me to Rev. Linward Crowe, a Presbyterian pastor who was then its president and has now worked with the Navigators in prison ministry in Philadelphia for many years. Through these meetings, I got to know what was happening on a broader governmental scale across the city as it impacted the faith community.

As a result, I was able to interact with Dr. Wilson Goode, then mayor of the city and an ordained clergyman, and he accepted my invitation to come and preach at the church where I was the pastor. We were able to form a new community group in my neighborhood called C.A.S.T – Communities and Schools Together. It was comprised of representatives from local and citywide government offices, local schools and churches.

There I interacted with school leaders and others from various faith groups to engage in dialogue about how to help meet students' needs. When Mayor John Street took office, he established the Mayor's Office of Faith-Based Initiatives, and our church was selected as the faith-based partner for the high school across the street, which had a student body of over 3,500 teenagers. So much of that was thanks to Bonnie opening up those first doors.

Working in teams with such collegial relationships truly enriched my life and ministry. The defining quality of these people is that they are about caring for the needs of the people they serve for the kingdom, not for their own ego. How refreshing!

Of course, there are lots of other women who deserve a special mention as well. Besides church pastors and preachers, there are many notable examples of outstanding clergywomen serving in educational institutions as theologians and professors, or as chaplains in either the military or healthcare settings.

These people and others like them look for opportunities to move qualified clergy – regardless of gender – into places of leadership and influence. They provide examples and approaches I've tried to emulate by suggesting other local clergywomen for committees and appointments when appropriate.

In 2017, for example, I completed my term on one of our district boards, a position I held for almost 20 years. The team is comprised of about 20 clergypersons, with only two females. But before I declined the nomination to continue for another four years, I had already given thought to the name of another clergywoman I could nominate to fill my spot.

She was asked. She accepted. And she now serves very proficiently on that board.

The point is that we can be purposeful by suggesting qualified females for all kinds of ministry positions when the environment around us is open to receive them. This is one way women can champion each other into places and positions where their voice is needed but has not previously been present.

Yes, it's great to have models and champions to support us. But sometimes they're not readily available. So who do you call when you're new or really lost about how to handle a person or situation? It's common for a leader to need more specific help at some time or another. This is where a third distinctive category of reinforcement becomes critical.

Mentors.

When Moses' hands grew tired, they took a stone and put it under him and he sat on it. Aaron and Hur held his hands up - one on one side, one on the other - so that his hands remained steady till sunset. So Joshua overcame the Amalekite army with the sword.

Exodus 17:12-13

CHAPTER 6

DRIVER'S ED

Help! I don't know what to do!

There have been numerous times over my years as a pastor when I needed someone to talk to openly, honestly and without judgment about personal issues, church situations, or even just questions about how to do something. When those moments come, it is such a gift to have a genuine mentor.

A mentor is that trusted counselor or guide who helps us navigate the way as we learn lessons and apply principles to the practice of ministry. That person who helps us make the journey from "readiness to effectiveness" as defined by Dr. Weems in chapter five. We may have more than one mentor, since they may come and go in and out of our lives as we grow and our needs change.

In his doctoral dissertation,[1] Dr. Mark Walker, the senior pastor of Spokane Valley Church of the Nazarene in Spokane Valley, Washington, defines mentoring as "a relationship of influence." He says that it's not "if" but "how" we influence, adding that the connection is more about formation than education. Because of the relationship's very nature, the person being mentored experiences a movement from knowledge to wisdom.

Walker suggests that there are several key areas of focus in a mentoring relationship:

- Character – the formation of a person
- Understanding vocational identity – what it means not just to do pastoral things, but to be a pastor (i.e. competence balanced with the ministry of presence)

- Practical skills – mastery of skills that create effectiveness (e.g., weekly rhythms and sermon preparation, leading corporate worship, directing board meetings, pastoral care, administration, discipleship, etc.)

- Reflection – a time to stop and think; having someone to talk with about experiences that are shaping the call, including times of disappointment or perceived failure. Walker says that having a trustworthy mentor provides a safe environment to do that.

My former senior pastor, Dr. Chuck Gates, has been my primary pastoral mentor throughout my ministry. A former missionary in South Africa with his wife Judy and their family, Chuck became my pastor upon returning to the United States. He holds a uniquely global view of ministry and a spirit for teaching that's had far-reaching effects.

At last count, there were approximately 37 ministers who have been under his mentorship who now serve in full-time ministry, including Pastor Dawn. I will be forever grateful to God that he came into my life when he did.

As I described in a previous chapter, Pastor Gates was the first person to recognize the evidence of God's call in my life. But he went so much further than that. He opened up a place for me to serve as the administrative pastor on staff in the local church, even giving away ministry opportunities so I myself could take on projects and ministries that would solidify my call and help me learn the ropes. Training me in the basics, he displayed daily that he wasn't intimidated by my strengths but willing to walk alongside me, teaching me how to put those gifts to effective use.

Along the way, we definitely did ride in cars together – with both our spouses in the know. I cannot imagine how different the shape of my ministerial life would be if we hadn't had those times to talk things over. They gave me so many opportunities to ask all the questions I had, including about my own spiritual growth and establishing a theology of holiness and pastoral practice. This one-to-one communication enhanced my progress as a pastor and leader.

Pastor Gates led me through the cross-cultural experience of shifting from business to ministry with great dedication and patience, holding a deep conviction that I would flourish as a pastor. Today, he's one of my best friends and a true brother, and we have an "iron sharpens iron" relationship that is so crucial for personal and spiritual development. It's yet another aspect of his faith in God, right along with how he and Judy lived through the untimely death of their daughter, Heather, who was about to graduate with her master's degree.

She had such a bright future ahead of her, but an unexpected illness swiftly took her life, leaving Chuck and Judy to continue on without her on this side of heaven. And continue they did, handling their pain with grace and leaning completely on the Lord for the day-by-day strength they needed.

I learned so much from them during that agonizing experience. I've learned so much from them in general. The greatest gift they have given me is just being themselves as they serve God wholeheartedly - in good times and in bad.

I worked as an associate pastor on staff with Pastor Gates for three years until I was offered the opportunity to become the senior pastor of a multi-ethnic urban church in northeast Philadelphia. But that didn't mean he was too far away if I needed him.

I vividly remember the first time I was required to perform a funeral service, a task I'd never had to do before as an administrative pastor. So I called him and admitted how lost I was about the process. "I have no idea what I'm doing here," I said. And so he guided me through it, from the length of the sermon to riding in the hearse with the funeral director.

Over the years, this mentor and friend has spent hours and hours investing himself in me. Without his input, I would not be who I am today.

He's one of the more significant influences in my pastoral journey, but there are plenty of other figures who should be noted as well. Proper credit, for instance, needs to go to the laity in local churches who hold a healthy view of women in general. In particular, I have met and interacted with plenty of male laity over the course of my ministry who value women's ideas, who can follow their lead, and who have given input and honest feedback that helped me grow as a person and professional.

There are other people who are typically open to such things, though I have to admit there are some places where I've bumped into roadblocks or been prevented from crossing certain lanes seemingly for the sole reason that I'm female. Even the best mentors could not have totally prepared me for those experiences.

Two of the most difficult "lane changes" I've faced dealt with money and authority.

In certain church assignments, I quickly came to realize that some of my predecessors had not understood finances very well, including budgeting, compensation and the like – skills that are not taught in seminary. Unfortunately, some had been poor stewards of finances. It's not that they did anything unethical or illegal, but they nonetheless did not use sound principles and practices that could protect the church. They just didn't know.

My business background had equipped me with those tools, yet when I began asking in-depth questions about stewardship of the church's money, I got some pushback. For some, it was simply because that was an unusual thing for any pastor to do. But I could tell that, for some male board members, having a woman question the money was unfamiliar too. This was not how things were done at home, where they were in charge of the family finances.

It took a while to gain trust and show that I knew what I was talking about, but I did eventually breakthrough the stereotype-driven mentalities at play. After that, they offered me great support and help in making sure things were done in accordance with sound procedures. For example, at one of those churches, the Treasurer and Finance Committee adopted a policy of using various methods to regularly communicate financial information to congregants, which gratefully relieved me of having to do this as the pastor.

But I still wanted to know what was going on at all times. I used to say that if someone was going to jail because of poor money handling, it would be me by virtue of my position as the pastor. And while we laughed, it was really no joke.

Another illustration of difficulty crossing the money lane happened when I, as a District staff person, asked one of the district boards to set aside funds in order to complete an initiative we were already working on. It would take several years and an investment of cash to make the dream come alive, and so I asked them to designate $300,000.

They gave an unequivocal no to that request.

Now, according to the Clifton StrengthsFinder assessment, two of my primary strengths are taking responsibility and achieving. When I feel like I'm up against a wall without the ability to employ either of those strengths, it becomes exhausting, both mentally and emotionally. And that was the case here.

I eventually left that position, burned out because the wonderful plans I believed God had for us couldn't be implemented without either an infusion of cash or a miracle, neither of which happened. Yet, later, a man was hired to replace me; and it wasn't long afterward that money began flowing into the very project I'd been turned down for.

What was the difference between him and me, I wondered? I genuinely try to be careful not to read into things or make assumptions, since that's not a healthy approach for anyone involved. Yet sometimes the evidence does point in specific directions.

To this day, I don't want to believe the board lacked confidence in my plan because of my gender. But I've never been sure.

The same questions apply to the time I led a proposal in a local church for a major project that involved more than a million dollars. Try as I did, I couldn't gain consensus no matter how much some of the leaders wanted to move ahead. Again, I can't say for certain; but I'm left speculating even now whether more progress would have been made had a man – even one with my exact same skills and approaches – been driving that initiative.

As for crossing the authority lane, I recall a time early in my ministerial life when I was asked to present a workshop for local pastors. It was on the topic of small-group development, something I had plenty of successful experience with between my years of corporate training and my own local church. So I was prepared and excited about this new opportunity.

Yet when I arrived, the vibe in the class was definitely off. I distinctly remember being about halfway through my allotted time when I realized that some of the senior members there were looking at me with disdain.

Immediately, my brain filled with questions even while I continued to speak.

What's wrong?

Is there food on my face?

Did I say something offensive?

Is the training off base?

The answer, however, turned out to be much more simple.

A colleague told me much later that some of the group members did not have a favorable perception of me that day. My lack of pastoral experience combined with my gender created barriers to their ability or willingness to receive what I was trying to teach.

My enthusiasm could not make up for their ideas about my qualifications, and I certainly couldn't change my gender. No matter that it had never even occurred to me that having a woman teach – especially one so new to the ministry – would be problematic. Another bump against culture. Women didn't hold the leadership power back then, some 20 years ago.

To a large degree, we still don't today.

And it can be difficult to learn how to navigate issues of power and authority in leadership if the concept of women leaders isn't positively ingrained in an organization or denomination's culture. Once I better understood the cultural context of my working environment, I was able to find joy and contentment regardless of whether I was leading up front or quietly in the background.

There are times when I am asked to take on initiatives and I go on to lead with full confidence, with others following. But I've also accepted that when I feel like people don't want or appreciate my leadership, God does. And my call to serve is first and foremost for the Lord, not everybody else. So, I keep leading where he shows me and when the opportunities arise.

This reminds me of a story from my days in junior high school. I was selected to play the violin in a new orchestra formed from students across the entire county of schools. If you know anything about playing the violin, you know it's almost always more fun to be in the first violin section. They get to play the melody line most of the time, while the second violin section gets the harmony parts.

It's beautiful when it comes together in a performance; but practicing those harmony parts alone in your room can be grueling.

My orchestra conductor, Mrs. Socolofsky, told me after tryouts that I made it into the first violin section. I was so excited! But then she surprised me by asking if I would instead play the first-chair position in the second violin section.

"Second violin!" I thought. "Ugh!"

She went on to explain that she needed a strong player who would lead the section, and she knew I was not afraid to play out. Now, that made sense to me. And her confidence in me made me feel like a strong leader in that orchestra, even if I was only in eighth grade!

I never forgot that lesson – that sometimes we are called on to lead from the second position. And we should give it all we've got.

I was fortunate to have this kind of female mentor who helped me learn some valuable lessons early in life. But in the church setting, where are the female leaders who will mentor women into the future?

That question especially applies to those who believe in the concept that only women can mentor women. I've had too many valuable male mentors to believe that's true. But even if it were, I didn't know of any accessible women doing what I was doing back when I started. Remember, the closest female pastor was over four hours away.

As the years went by though, more and more women began to come through our district's credentials board seeking ordination. According to the prevailing mindset, the ministry board's logical move was to tell them to call me for mentoring. I once returned from vacation to find a note from my administrative assistant that said, "You must be popular!" Attached were five messages from women in my local area who'd been told to call me for mentoring.

Five.

In addition, each of them needed something different and was at a different stage of their ministerial journey. There was no way I could mentor everyone who asked me; and while I tried to create a cohort group, we never really came together. It just didn't work out, and no wonder. Suitable mentorship requires proper time and attention to build a relationship, something the ministry board knew.

Problem was, they also "knew" that women were supposed to mentor women.

Maybe that concept could work better if there were more tenured female pastors with enough experience to take on such positions. And maybe it could work out if there were more places for women to serve in senior leadership roles – places where they could gain experience in the first place.

Then again, maybe we're complicating a matter that doesn't need to be complicated.

To be honest, it's been a gift to be mentored, championed and befriended by my male counterparts, as they're the ones who largely make up the ministry culture I'm immersed in. As such, knowing them and understanding how they operate helps me be the most effective leader I can in my context.

Moreover, men shouldn't fear building godly relationships with females in ministry. They can intentionally ask women about their experiences with an open mind and try to understand their point of view and how they arrived at their conclusions. Men can listen and engage, looking for places where a woman's gifts and talents can be applied.

They can, and many of them do.

I wish some women would stop automatically assuming that all male clergy are our adversaries. They're not. Some are trying very hard to help us, but they may not know how or what exactly we need. We should try to find them in our networks. Who are they? Who is a model for you in particular? Who are the champions of women? Who might be able to mentor you in some aspect of ministry?

And once you have identified those answers, ask yourself this critical question: *Am I really ready to be mentored*?

I've had the opportunity to mentor both male and female clergy over the years. The process is very individual and can be a lot of fun. However, I've also tried to mentor people who really didn't want to be mentored. Some had such a long list of what they wanted that I, at least, couldn't possibly fulfill their needs.

Dr. Gates taught his leaders-in-training to look for F.A.T. Christians: those who are faithful, available and teachable. I've found this to be a good tool when choosing who to mentor. A person who is not teachable is hard to guide. In their minds, they've already figured it all out for themselves and they don't really want help. Therefore, taking them on is not only a waste of my time but also theirs.

We should always choose carefully who we invest ourselves in. This doesn't mean we ignore people who ask for help; it means we're honest on whether we can actually provide that help and whether they are willing to receive it.

There's also a difference between formal and informal mentoring. Formal mentoring has a defined plan and goals that are the focus of the experience. Informal mentoring happens more through "catching" what someone is doing by spending time with them or watching them and asking lots of questions.

In my final year at my most recent pastoral assignment, our church was fortunate to have a young man come to serve as associate pastor, the second male staff member to work with me there. In his interview, it became clear that Rev. Tim Hahn, a recent seminary graduate, was a good scholar and theologian. I told him before he came that while I love to think about and discuss theology, as a pastor, I excel more as a practitioner.

Knowing this, Pastor Tim took in everything he could about local church pastoral work in his year with us. In exchange, I learned everything I could from him about theology and how pastors from a younger generation and mindset think! With both of us eager to acquire more knowledge and experience, we had a wonderful, mutual exchange of ideas and we both learned a lot working together.

It's so important to never stop growing, never stop learning from others, and never assume that someone else can't teach us new things. Especially if their experience, age, gender or nationality is different than ours.

I tell the clergy I mentor to watch for opportunities to participate and learn, and to invite themselves in when possible to work alongside good role models or mentors of either gender. This might begin with something as easy as purposefully sitting at a table mixed with male and female clergy at meetings instead of forming a women-only or men-only group.

Women specifically can also accept offers to preach and be willing to serve on a board or committee if those opportunities come up - even if they're the only females represented. These are simple methods that can integrate men and women in order to create an exchange of ideas and teachings. And many women are waiting to be asked by the powers that be.

If you're someone who is responsible to fill board or other leadership positions, perhaps you can think of ways to balance the power and authority between the genders – with qualified people, of course, not just elevating individuals based on gender alone. An intentional effort is needed in this regard. These experiences help equip mentors for future generations.

Actually, many people are privileged to have personal mentors even as young children. No matter if we recognize these figures as such right away, we can look back and see the impact they had on us during our formative years. It's good to name these individuals and recognize the contributions they made to our lives. After all, they shaped us in meaningful ways.

We can do the same for others by setting the same kind of loving standards. The truth is that young people are watching us whether we like it or not. Our example tells them something about us and the God we serve.

There are mentors and potential mentors all around us. Sometimes, we just need to think outside of the box, recognizing that some may be people we will never actually meet. In his business-minded book, *Your One Word*, Evan Carmichael calls them aspirational mentors. He writes:

> Aspirational mentors are people who you look up to
> and learn from. They are people you've never met but
> might one day. Some of them might be dead, but you
> can still learn from their success.[2]

Going by that clear definition, most people can name at least a few aspirational mentors, including those outside the church. Perhaps it's the coach of a professional sports team, a business owner, or a renowned scholar or theologian. Even though you only know this person from a distance, the sum total of their life has still impacted yours.

I have so many of these that I can't name them all in a single chapter. But one example of my female aspirational mentors is Catherine Wilkes Booth, who - with her husband, William - started the Salvation Army in 1865. She was a fiery preacher who knew without a doubt the call of God on her life. So preach she did!

Oh, how I wish I could have been in a meeting to hear one of her sermons firsthand!

Catherine was an advocate who boldly professed the Biblical teaching that women in ministry are equals with men. The things I've read about her encouraged me to stand courageously in the pulpit and be confident in God's calling. She has given me my all-time favorite quote: "If we are to better the future, we must disturb the present."

I can think of others I've met through their written works, like Henri Nouwen, Hannah Whitall Smith, Dietrich Bonhoeffer and Oswald

Chambers. Then there are people whose actions inspire me, like Rosa Parks and Dr. Martin Luther King, Jr. I could go on and on with examples of both men and women who have taught me life lessons, been spiritual teachers, and shaped and formed various aspects of my life in different periods of my personal development, which continues even now.

Some of the people I've talked about in this chapter have become my dear friends. Others remain mentors from a distance. But whichever they are – model, champion or mentor – my ministerial life has been enriched because of their example. I pray that every male and female leader will be surrounded by people like this... and then become a similar example for someone else.

That's what God called us to do. To be.

That's what He did for us.

We are fortunate to have people who can inspire us to be all we can be; but the ultimate role model, of course, is Jesus Christ. From Him, we learn and appreciate all the attributes of holy, unconditional love that are elusive to us without knowing His great affection for us. As we see His life presented in Scripture, Jesus becomes our mentor, model, champion, advocate and friend. We are created in His image, and He loves us like no one on Earth can.

Again, thanks be to God!

CHAPTER 7

BUMPS IN THE ROAD

My cell phone rang one afternoon: a call from a clergywoman who participated in a cohort I led. And she was clearly struggling.

"I need someone to talk to," she said through sniffles. "Do you have a minute?"

Through her sobs, she relayed how, that morning, a family member caught her by surprise by criticizing her for accepting the senior pastor's offer to preach in his place on a Sunday when he planned to be away. A person this woman thought was supportive of her call to ministry had said things that left her devastated.

This kind of response hurts especially when it comes from our closest loved ones. And while she knew they were only expressing their opinion, it dug deep.

To make matters worse, it came from another woman.

Clergywomen are sadly mistaken if they think everyone will be overjoyed that they followed God's call into ministry. I could name other female colleagues who have cried the same tears of pain as comments from family, friends and other clergy members – even in denominations that say they support women in ministry – wound their psyche and hurt their heart. And a typical response for these women is often to "just suck it up" since, as they've already learned, it's not easy to change someone's mind about whether a woman can preach or be a pastor.

I once was interviewed for a pastoral position by a church board that had wisely prepared questions ahead of time for each board member to ask me. As soon as the interview began, I noticed that one man had his Bible open in front of him. Sure enough, when it was his turn, he laid his hands on the exposed pages and said in an accusatory tone, "What gives you the right to think you can come here to be our pastor?"

Those may not have been his precise words, but they're close, and I knew exactly what he was asking. My district superintendent, who was also at the interview, was surprised by both the question and the insensitive way it had been asked. He immediately spoke up to remind the man that our denomination has always ordained women and that women hold all kinds of leadership positions, including that of a pastor. I then followed up with my own answer, which was to explain more about my call and that I had already been a pastor for over 15 years in another setting.

In the end, that church did ask me to be their pastor, and I served there for nine great years. But it was not long after I arrived that this gentleman left the church. He just did not believe that women could serve in pastoral leadership. To his credit, he did stay for a few months to hear me preach. He took time to give it a chance, but it was just not for him.

As the pastor, I respected him for holding to his convictions. I felt sure he was basing his actions on his sincere interpretation of Scripture, and I think it's better for someone to leave being true to their beliefs than to stay and cause problems or remain unhappy. But not everyone in the congregation understood my position on the matter. Some on the board even asked me to "go after him". Obviously, they sensed his discomfort and wanted to make things right and keep him in the church. He was their friend and brother in Christ.

But I knew.

You just can't change someone's mind that easily.

Each of us lives with distinct mental models, those ideas and assumptions that aren't a conscious part of our thinking yet still shape how we understand and respond to the world around us. These are paradigms – worldviews that provide the framework for how we perceive and understand things. Every church or denomination has paradigms by which it understands its ministry, develops its programs and expresses its faith. And when these mental models are challenged or collapse, there is a cycle of grief before acceptance sets in to allow a new way of thinking.

While sharing insights from his own journey, pastor and author Brian McLaren refers to a comment from psychiatrist Dr. M. Scott Peck, renowned author of *The Road Less Traveled*. Peck says "that depression often accompanies the collapse of a mental map or paradigm; it is a natural and necessary expression of grief; grief over the loss of something perhaps as dear to us as a brother or mother; our worldview, our way of seeing life."[1]

So it's easy to see why a mindset that's been developed over the years and reinforced by one's belief about roles, culture and even Biblical interpretations is difficult to change. For years, God's people sang on Sunday morning, "Change my heart, O God, make it ever new."[2] But for many, change didn't come.

As related to women being called to full-time ministry, there are still deeply held convictions in the church about our role as pastors, preachers and leaders – even if they're not spoken aloud. True change on this subject can only come by the intervention of the Holy Spirit and a mind and spirit that is willing to "learn, unlearn and relearn," as famed businessman Alvin Toffler would say. [3]

There are also many people who unknowingly make backhanded compliments to female clergy. So many things have been said to me over the years that were meant to be nice, yet came across exactly the opposite. That's why I decided early on in ministry that it's always best to focus on the intentions behind a statement and to respond with thoughtful answers. Otherwise, it's too easy to be injured.

Some comments, like the one my friend at the beginning of the chapter received, are intended to correct or offer truth as that person understands it. The person making them might not actually see how offensive they're being. For instance, I remember a conversation I had at a conference with a male colleague I greatly respected as a churchman. During our lunch discussion, he told me, "You know, I don't really believe in women in ministry. But if I did, I think I could have you as my pastor."

Perhaps there's something about having lunch at conferences that brings out these conversations? Regardless, I choked on my ham sandwich, smiled politely and thanked him for the compliment, which I knew is what he intended – even though it came across in a backhanded way. Really, I was too surprised to challenge him on why he didn't believe in women clergy in the first place.

That was the first time it even occurred to me that, even in a denomination that's ordained women since its inception over 100 years ago, there are still some – even elders – who aren't fully on board.

Thankfully, the Holy Spirit took care of changing this particular brother's heart and mind. He is now a strong advocate for clergywomen in leadership. But at the time, steeped in his opinion of the truth, he didn't think he was being offensive. And I needed to consider his intentions just as much as my reaction.

Another example of a backhanded – or perhaps just thoughtless – compliment came from a woman from one of our local churches. At the time, I held a position of visibility as our district's urban mission director. She was excited about my leadership role and tried to compliment me by saying, "Oh Shirley, you're our Sarah Palin!"

It was an election year. And little did she know that I was not a fan of said person, no disrespect to those who are. So it took me a second to process through my offense to understand what she meant. It quickly dawned on me that she was trying to say she saw me as a female leader and role model for her and other women on the district, so I thanked her for her kind intentions.

Ultimately, those kinds of "compliments" don't bother me because I know the people who offer them have their heart in the right place. She was an advocate! Though it just goes to show how easily we can assume that we all think alike just because we like each other or are both Christians.

It's better to give grace when such words come our way: to listen between the lines and receive the intention of the person's heart. Rather than be offended at our differing political interpretations, I chose to see it as being compared to someone she admired.

The same is true when congregants or visitors say, "That was a nice talk, Pastor" after I just preached my heart out. How often I have wanted to respond, "No, that was not *a talk*, that was *a sermon!*"

I used to think that comments like this from a parishioner offered clues as to how they were responding to me as a woman preacher. It might be the first time they have ever heard a woman preach, and I've discovered that some people just don't know what to say. They may not know if it's appropriate to acknowledge that I just preached a sermon. In any event, this particular kind of feedback always struck me as another of those backhanded compliments. But I've since learned that this statement is also made to male preachers. That's right – it was my paradigm that had to change on this one!

It's easy to make wrong assumptions, and if we don't listen carefully enough to people's hearts as well as their words, well-intended comments can wound us unnecessarily. As for those times when a person's words or actions do offend us or cause us pain, we can look to God to soothe our hurting hearts.

Because he knows.

Even when we're left completely perplexed by what we take in, he knows.

That includes how, during my church experience, I've largely felt much higher expectations from other women than those from men – something I've never really figured out. Although I try to believe that other women are my advocates, their words, behaviors and expectations toward me have often felt antagonistic. And I know for sure that I am not the only clergywoman who experiences this.

In general, I've had a much more difficult time learning how to effectively lead women in the church than men. It's much more likely for a female congregant to take me to task than their male counterparts. There have been unjust criticisms, and even emotional and verbal abuse directed at me by other women. This includes mean emails sent directly to me... unkind words spoken about me in the foyer... things said behind my back that then made their way to my ears.

And, unfortunately, I have to admit that there were times in the past that I too was not as kind and encouraging to other women as I should have been. *I had to learn how much we need each other's support.*

Perhaps there's a broader issue here that faces females in ministerial leadership. In a *Christianity Today* article, author and researcher Halee Gray Scott highlights the findings of a State of Pastors report conducted by the Barna Group, an evangelical Christian polling firm. Her resulting commentary included how:

> Though most pastors, regardless of gender, are satisfied with their roles, female pastors are more likely than male pastors to wish they had been more prepared for the expectation [that] they "must do everything" and "must do it perfectly." [4]

Furthermore, the Barna Group found that female pastors are more likely than male pastors to report that congregants' comments on their leadership were "critical," "judging," and "unhelpful."

I wish it didn't, but this resonates with me – specifically when it comes to women.

There was the time my husband and I made a total of three one-hour round trips – two of them in one day – to a store to purchase new curtains meant to replace ones that covered a certain storage area in the church. The old ones had been hanging in this highly visible location for more than 20 years. Maybe this wasn't something I should have taken on. But I was tired of looking at the dirty things, and we were purchasing new furniture for the room at the time. So, I genuinely thought that replacing the curtains would be a positive change. I didn't know who else to ask to handle the task, and it seemed easy enough to do.

When the first two pairs went up, there was an obvious and immediate problem. The length of the curtains didn't match even though they weren't labeled as seconds. That's why we had to make multiple trips: to return and try another pair. Additionally, since he's a carpenter, Ron even went so far as to figure out how to create a new rod that would allow proper entrance to the items stored behind the curtains. Then he hung it carefully, guiding me as we discussed how to make this work for everyone who needed access.

All of that careful consideration and work didn't make the curtains hang evenly though. So, late on Saturday afternoon, having spent most of the day trying to get them right, I said, "Let's just leave it for tomorrow. I'll go back next week to get ones that work."

The next day after the worship service, other women soundly criticized me because the curtains looked so terrible. The hems weren't straight, obviously; and apparently, I didn't know how to hang drapes correctly.

The comments were sharp and hard to hear. No one asked me what happened or if the curtains would stay that way or if I was still working on them. The assumption was that I didn't know how bad they looked. I went home after church that day hurt and bewildered, and I cried. So much effort. So little appreciation. No offer to help. Only God knew everything we'd done to try and get ready for Sunday.

But yes, God really did know. And in the end, that was enough.

There are simply times when a leader, male or female, has to fall back on that fact alone. No one other than Ron and God ever knew that my feelings had been hurt so much by the remarks directed at me that day. And I believe, in this case, that's how it was supposed to be. We can't expect others to understand all we handle or why we handle it all. I honestly don't believe those comments were meant to upset me, even though they did.

Curtains aside, other women have called me a control freak and told me I'm so uptight about worship services that I wouldn't know how to make room for the Spirit to work. I've also been spoken to like I was ignorant or a child, verbally abused and emotionally sabotaged.

If that sounds bad, that's because sometimes it was.

But let me assure you: There are also many wonderful people – both women and men – who have championed my cause, prayed for me with diligence and passion, loved me when I wasn't perfect, laughed with me until we cried, and been there for me as colleagues and friends in both my best and darkest times.

There have also been definite moments where I've received kindness and affirmation, like with the woman who often told me, "I'm so excited to have a woman pastor!" Another female took it upon herself to be my prayer warrior. This kind of support from other women in particular is both meaningful and deeply appreciated. And numerous strong women leaders have supported my call for many years.

I thank God for every one of them.

That's why, as I've learned, it's not just about trying to recognize where the other person is coming from, as discussed earlier. It's also important for leaders to know themselves. We need to know our strengths, capabilities and limits. Our emotions and triggers... And then we have to learn how to operate in our strengths, manage our emotions and enlist others in the areas where we're weakest.

Apparently, church curtain-choosing was not my forte even though we finally did get them right. As such, if I had it to do over, I would have left the old dirty drapes hanging even though they were more embarrassing to me than one morning of new curtains with unmatched hems. Which brings me to another point...

In a volunteer setting, as many churches are, there is not always someone willing or available to take care of ordinary or mundane tasks. There's no hiring reliable people with dependable schedules or, for that matter, firing those who don't work out. The reality is that some people help a lot, some don't know how to help, and others just don't want to. And no one can be forced to do something if they don't want to.

As such, there may not be someone with the necessary skills to complete the task at hand. So, because you are the pastor, sometimes it's you and you alone left to change the drapes (or not change the drapes), fix the toilet or clean the foyer, talking to Jesus as you do. I think this is probably true for male pastors too.

As it relates to women specifically, however, there are many encouraging New Testament stories of how Jesus behaved toward women. His treatment of them as described in the Bible is a true role model for us today.

Those who were treated with scorn or disdain by others were offered grace and compassion from Jesus. The sisters, Mary and Martha, received sound instruction on how to live and direct their focus to the most important thing. His treatment of the woman caught in adultery included accountability and compassion. And remember, Jesus was left alone with her. Yikes!

For that matter, he was also alone with the Samaritan woman at the well when he encountered her and revealed himself to her, and he was alone with Mary in the garden after his resurrection. Overall, the way Jesus dealt with women is inspiring.

We are valuable in his eyes.

When we read the accounts of these and other women in Scripture, we are affirmed in knowing that we are created in God's image and loved deeply by Christ himself. The recognition of how cherished we are to him – male or female, pastor or not – will hold us steady through many times of testing or difficulties. God's unconditional love for us is powerful. And there seems to be a connection between grasping the "agape" love God has for us with our capacity to love God, others and self.

When questioned by the religious teachers of the day about what is the greatest commandment, Jesus referenced a passage from the Torah as recorded in Deuteronomy 6:4-5. The words are known as the "Shema," which means to hear or listen. They were very familiar to those who were asking. As recorded in Matthew 22:37-40, Jesus told them:

> …'Love the Lord your God with all your heart and with all your soul and with all your mind.' This is the first and greatest commandment. And the second is like it: 'Love your neighbor as yourself.' All the Law and the Prophets hang on these two commandments.

Even though we love Christ and are called to love our neighbor, including our adversaries, the greatest challenge may be to learn how to establish proper self-love: a way of loving ourselves with the love of Christ. It seems to me that this is a key part of this commandment. How can I love someone else if I don't know how to love myself?

This is not prideful or egotistical love I'm talking about. It's the love of God that embodies compassion and wonder and all the potential God sees in us. We love others as we love ourselves.

We would do well to reread I Corinthians 13, known as the "love chapter", and apply it to ourselves. Like this:

Love is patient – Are you patient with yourself?

Love is kind – How about it? Do you waver in being kind to yourself?

Love keeps no record of wrongs – How are you doing with that one?

Love does not dishonor others, is not self-seeking or easily angered; it keeps no record of wrongs...

You can take it from here.

Satan is the father of lies and our greatest adversary and he will use other people to get at us physically, mentally, emotionally and spiritually. He will also mess with our heads and offer false notions about who we are as the sons and daughters of God. And when we are running on all cylinders, tired or discouraged, we might be tempted to ask – "who's got my back?" But Scripture is clear that we have the advocate of all advocates.

His name is Jesus.

When we don't know how to advocate for ourselves, he does it for us. He opens the door and invites us in, and he is the one driver we should be thrilled to sit next to. He will navigate the way as we pursue his call on our life.

CHAPTER 8

ALTERNATE ROUTES

It was a definite "ah-ha!" moment.

In the spring of 2015, a group of Wesleyan Holiness Women Clergy, of which I am a member, met at a retreat center in North Carolina for our biannual conference. About 400 clergywomen came together to worship, learn, have fun and reconnect with friends. It was here that I attended a full day workshop with the hefty title "The Trinity, Subordinationism and Women in Ministry: New Doctrinal Deviations in Evangelicalism."

That title alone intrigued me enough to find out what it was about.

Everyone who sat in on the session was exposed to rich teaching that day. For me in particular, it was the first time I heard two terms that would go on to become very meaningful to me: *complementarian* and *egalitarian*. These words describe two distinct biblically based points of view about the roles of men and women.

A narrow definition of the complementarian position incorporates the belief that women are not permitted to serve in pastoral leadership or hold any leadership authority over a man, including in the marriage relationship. The egalitarian stance endorses equality of both males and females in all leadership roles. It's easy to see how such diverse views could result in controversy.

As I struggled that day to listen and rapidly take notes, the theological implications of what I was hearing astounded me. "How can it be that this is the first time I've heard this?" I thought. I felt like I had missed a major road sign on my ministerial journey! I remember thinking that, surely, somewhere along my then-20 years in pastoral ministry, I would have heard these terms and understood them more clearly.

As it turned out, I was relieved to hear that the terminology was relatively new. Yet new or not, what I learned that day brought so many of my experiences into perspective.

Let me explain…

I had never considered opinions that either oppose or affirm women in leadership or authority in the church were tied to a question of such theological depth. I always thought people came to their conclusions because of their culture or upbringing, or their interpretation of passages in the Bible about women. That's all. But in this workshop, the nature of the controversy was presented in light of how the two positions theologically approach the Trinity, primarily in the relationship between Jesus Christ and God the Father.

What, if any, implications do these different points of view have on human relationships, especially between men and women or husbands and wives?

Are both genders really equal in every sense? And what does that mean exactly?

There has been a theological debate for centuries over scriptural interpretation of the biblical roles of men and women, both in the home and church. But what are the practical implications of these beliefs?

For example, in what ways can a woman function and still be in line with God's Word? Can she lead, teach, preach, etc.? Or is her role to assist the males around her through submission to their leadership in every regard?

Stated another way, is it possible for males and females to be equal in essence (created equally in God's sight), but NOT in function (having different roles to play in this life)?

Culturally, most people have encountered this debate on some level, such as whether girls can play football with boys or join the previously all-male military academies. And it's not uncommon to encounter opposing viewpoints and attitudes that trigger big conflicts about what is the "right" answer. While it can be hard to find consensus about these everyday life issues, it's even harder in the church where strongly held beliefs are based on whatever an individual, or even a denomination, holds as correct biblical interpretation.

I have definitely come up against both sides of the debate as a female in ministry.

What shook me that day at the workshop though was the explanation of how, in theological terms, the larger controversial question, at its core, is whether God the Father and God the Son (Jesus) are fully equal in both essence (their being) AND their function as God, or are they only equal in essence with distinctive functions?

To put it more simply, is God the Father superior over Jesus in some way even though Jesus is God in the flesh? And if so, what are the implications of that for the practical relationships between men and women?

The idea of a hierarchy is important to this conversation. Hierarchy has to do with ranking, order, systems, chains of command, and who has control over what. Ultimately, who's in charge? Even though I had heard discussions about relational hierarchy before as it relates to men and women, this was the first time I heard it explained as it applies to the concept of Trinity.

And here is where my interest was really piqued as the two main views of the debate were presented. [1]

The complementarian stance was described as maintaining that an eternal hierarchy exists in authority between what Christians recognize as the three persons of the Trinity – God the Father, God the Son (Jesus) and God the Holy Spirit. In this view, the Father is seen as the highest-ranking member, and the Son and Spirit are subordinate to him and submit to his authority.

Egalitarians, on the other hand, maintain that all three persons of the Trinity are eternally equal in their authority in both essence and function, and that the ways in which Jesus is portrayed in Scripture as being subordinate to the Father are related specifically to His mission of redemption and incarnation.

Things got more interesting from there as I quickly saw the connection between these theological perspectives and how they translate into the day-to-day workings of gender in relationships.

Because, based on these views, it follows that complementarians also believe that there is a hierarchy between men and women, with women being created equal to men in value but subordinate in their role. Egalitarians, meanwhile, hold the opposing view that males and females are created equal in authority both in their essence and in how they function.

Wow! Definitely two distinct ways of thinking about this topic.

Our workshop leaders went on to explore the implications of these two poles of belief, explain the theological points of agreement, and discuss hermeneutics (how a text is interpreted). We also delved into the role of history, the main ideas of both points of view, what scriptures are used by each to support their perspective, and the practical consequences for women in ministry today. We heard about implications that affect prayer, worship and praise, order or leadership structure, the family and church government.

By the end of the day, my mind was whirling with this new knowledge and my own related experiences. Frankly, as I later tried to study more about these ideas, I became overwhelmed by the volume and complexity of writings out there.

So why bring this up here at all?

Because I, and many other women ministers I know, have run up against the complementarian view that it is not appropriate for women to hold church leadership roles if they involve teaching or authority over men. This includes being a pastor or deacon, a ruling elder, or even a teacher of a class in which men are students.

And sadly, in my experience at least, many of the people who have opposed me in church leadership have not been able to support their arguments soundly with Scripture. Such ill-informed opposition presents a definite dilemma for those who are called, not to mention how very discouraging it can be when it sideswipes us.

Like the time my husband and I stopped at a Christian bookstore on the way home from a retreat. This store had an expansive selection of items compared to anywhere near where we lived, and I was looking for a particular book. A young female clerk sat on the floor, opening boxes of new merchandise. When I asked her for help, she stood up and said, "Why do you want that particular resource?"

Ron, being the proud spouse, said, "Oh, she's a minister!"

And that was all it took. A blistering tirade ensued when she told me in no uncertain terms that I COULD NOT BE A MINISTER – "IT IS UNBIBLICAL FOR WOMEN TO LEAD IN THE CHURCH."

I was shocked at the ferocity of her words – it was as if I was being condemned to hell! Her tone of voice certainly made it clear how strongly she felt about my profession. This was the first time I had been attacked like this in public, and it was intense.

I took a deep breath – under which I was thinking, "I just came here to buy a book, lady!" – and bit my tongue as she rang up the purchase and took my payment. Ron just stood by my side, understandably not knowing what to say.

When we left, I asked him to never tell anyone again that I was a pastor.

In the moment, I was angry with that young woman for being so rude. But after my anger subsided, I just felt sorry for her. I thought, "Lord, I hope you never call her into full time ministry because she won't know what to do!"

It seemed terrible to me that someone so young could have such a strong point of view that would hold her back from celebrating the call of God on some women's lives. And I hoped that she had come to her conclusions through a private study of Scripture, not just what others told her about it.

Being new to the ministry at the time, I didn't know yet how to address her kind of comments. And, honestly, even years later, I likely would not have argued back in such a public forum with such angry opposition.

But after attending that previously described workshop, I understood her position better and can now put words to her point of view. Very helpful indeed! Plus, I left grateful for the strong egalitarian position of my denomination and with a better understanding of how to articulate what I believe. And it further convinced me of how my own position on this subject reflects Jesus' teachings.

I also began to realize that there are many women like me who do not know about these ideas and could use the information/educational tools to assist them when they encounter adversaries who want to deny them their place in ministry.

I recently asked a seminary professor, one who is a clergywoman herself and deeply involved in women's mentoring, if her educational institution addressed these terms in the classroom. I was curious to know if young men and women coming through the school would be introduced to them and offered the opportunity to discuss the two poles of thought. It seems to me that this would prepare ministers-in-training for the opposition they will surely face from many Christians, laypeople and clergy alike.

However, the reply I got was that, to her knowledge, these two terms were not specifically addressed as any part of a formal curriculum. They might be presented or discussed informally, but there is no current requirement to bring them up. Other seminaries might promote an understanding of the subject. I don't know. But such institutions do seem like a great place to make sure the dialogue happens.

I recall an interaction I once had with a male pastor who I met in an ecumenical pastors' group in the town where we served. The group was a mix of strong complementarians and a few egalitarian pastors. At one of our meetings, this pastor led the prayer for our group and, in it, referred to "the men in this room" while I and another woman sat at the table.

When he finished, another male pastor who was sitting next to me turned and asked, "Did you hear his prayer?"

"Yes," I replied, "but I'm not going to say anything about it."

"That's okay," he said, "because I am!"

At another meeting a few months later, the young man who prayed that day came up to me to apologize and let me know that he hadn't even realized what he'd said. "I do tend to be a complementarian," he explained.

At the time, I didn't know exactly what that meant – but now I do!

I thought about how this same group of pastors had struggled to invite me into their ranks until I finally told the leader that if their group was an exclusive one, I didn't want to be a part of it anyway. That's when they finally asked me in. Of course, I have no proof that my gender was the issue. But looking back, I think it was.

To be honest, I never did find a good fit there regardless. I talked with the group leader about this but came to realize that sometimes men just don't get how awkward it feels to be treated differently. And in all fairness, some did go out of their way to make sure I was included, especially said leader, who is now a friend of mine.

After the men in the group got to know me better, they did ask me to let them know when they were being gender exclusive either in language or activities. On the one hand, I deeply appreciated their desire to know. On the other hand, it was uncomfortable having to be the one to bring up these issues all the time.

In my experience, women are darned if they do and darned if they don't. It's a lose-lose. If you say nothing, you're told you can't complain because you didn't speak up. Yet, if you do speak up, you're asked why you are so sensitive.

The implied message is often to get over it and move on.

Certainly, there are times when I do that. And certainly, there are times when I – and everyone else, male or female – should. But there are also times when something needs to be said because that's the only way to shape an awareness of exclusive language or behavior. On those occasions, I tried to express some of the ways that felt exclusive, even when the responses I got back were ones of bewilderment that said, "I don't get what you're talking about."

Another time, I was asked to preach at a Sunday-evening service at a local church where I knew many of the members. It was early in my ministerial journey, and I was thrilled to have the opportunity to bring God's Word to his people. That night, however, was my first experience having a man walk out of the church when he found out a woman was preaching.

Much later on, even while I wrote this book, I preached at another local church for a pastor who was on vacation, only to find out later that one of the female board members had stayed out of the sanctuary because a woman was preaching.

A female.

A board member.

So yes, we still have a way to go on this one.

While over the years, many church members have been very supportive of me as a pastor, I mentioned earlier that I have also lost church members because of their opposition to women in leadership. That's why, every time I was interviewed for a pastoral position, I told the board before they hired me that some people would never attend the church if they had a woman pastor. This dynamic is one that's unique to female clergy. A person might walk out because they don't like a male pastor's preaching style, looks, way of dressing, or even his ethnicity, but they won't be likely to leave *just because he's a man*.

Not so for a woman.

Clergy, both male and female, will repeatedly run into people who hold the complementarian interpretation of Scripture even if those people aren't aware that there's a name for what they believe. Even laity, especially those who have a woman pastor at their church, will also be confronted by arguments that renounce their pastor's authority and role. That's why, after that workshop, I also began to pay more attention to the materials churches use to teach lay classes.

Studies by authors and teachers who are of the complementarian position abound and are used regularly in egalitarian settings. Upon my arrival as pastor at one church, I asked one of our women's groups to stop using a particular Bible teaching series for this very reason. They thought I was crazy and controlling. But what are the implications for men and women who participate in these studies? I want to reinforce a different message about women, the message I believe is Biblical and held by those who believe in women in leadership!

Some egalitarian pastors commonly quote blogs, books and podcasts on social media published by complementarian authors, presenting them as cutting edge voices that should be listened to or read regularly. And while many of the insights are very good ones, I have to wonder if we are being careful with these tools. With so many good resources available to us, are we choosing with discretion? Look, I'm not saying the presenters aren't good, they are. I've quoted from them myself. But when people are studying *regularly* from teachings that don't support your position – either way – why not find ones that do?

Clergywomen are also affected by complementarian views when trying to gain a place to serve or when being offered jobs at less-than-a-man's pay. For my first position as an associate pastor, I received no benefits and a very small salary – about one-third of what I had been earning in my business. At the time, my husband and I had a daughter in college and our only other source of income was worker's compensation insurance benefits, since Ron had been injured on the job and could not work at his trade at that time.

This meant a significant loss of income for us, as he was a well-paid union worker with an amazing benefit package.

Three years later, when I left that pastoral position, a young man who was also going into ministry for the first time was offered the job as my replacement. That was when one of the church board members questioned how he would be able to support his family on such a low wage. "He has kids after all, and a wife to support."

It did not occur to this person that I was in the same situation – that I had a mortgage and a daughter in college. The only difference was that he was a man and thus viewed as responsible to take care of his family. I was present in the room for this discussion and, when one of the other board members asked my opinion on what I thought the job was worth, I could not even speak. It hurt me deeply.

Another time, a male pastor contacted me when he was surprised by one of his female board members who refused to give a young woman in their church her first local license so she could begin the path towards ordination. He wrongly assumed that women would automatically be advocates for one another. I sent him some helpful material to use, and after reviewing it, he was prepared to address her concerns at the next board meeting with Scripture and an overview of our beliefs.

Yet the Holy Spirit had spoken to this board member in the interim, and she came to the next meeting apologetic, making the motion to approve the license. Never underestimate the power of the Holy Spirit to change hearts and minds!

Then again, sometimes God works in less mysterious ways. Sometimes all you need is a random prompting.

If you are a pastor or church member, would you stop and take a look around at the various boards in your churches or denominational groups? What is the percentage of male to female? What is the ratio of male to female pastors in your community, across denominations or in non-denominational settings?

And when women sit on boards or committees, are they listened to and respected for the ideas and solutions they bring? Do you help facilitate that? Is the compensation fair and equitable between men and women on your staff? Do you speak up if it's not?

Or try this...

If you regularly attend a church, close your eyes and imagine it's Sunday morning. Cars are driving into the parking lot. People are coming through the doors and gathering together. The coffee is on. Perhaps Sunday School classes are getting ready to start or worship service is beginning.

Do you see it? Do you see your church on Sunday morning?

Now, remove all the women from the picture. That's right, take them out.

Take out the female preachers, teachers, board members and ministry leaders.

Do you see the loss?

Jim Henderson, in his book *The Resignation of Eve* gave it the subtitle: *What if Adam's Rib is No Longer Willing to Be the Church's Backbone?* Henderson paints a picture of such a void as he proposes that women are leaving the church in droves because they cannot find a meaningful place to serve with the gifts and talents God has given them. He says that women:

> *...often leave the relationship before they leave the room.* Their hearts precede their feet. Sometimes they don't even know that they're getting ready to leave. They're experiencing what I call resignation creep.[2]

This is reminiscent of the process of divorce, where one person proactively leaves the relationship first in an emotional sense before they physically remove themselves. And it happens for many reasons. As Henderson correctly argues, "So often it seems *it's not the work but the workers* who discourage us from wanting to try again. Another loss for the Kingdom."

Maybe you've never thought about the significant influence of the women in your church, whether clergy or lay minister. But I hope that Henderson's words will help us all to find the women who need guidance, mentoring or just encouragement. It's amazing how a simple compliment – "I see the Spirit of God in you" or "Your gifts and talents are so evident when you serve" – can shape a mindset of acceptance and love. This is especially important for young women who need to be set free to use their gifts, express their call, and be encouraged to find their place as a leader.

This can be as simple as recommending relevant reading material to them. There are so many sources of help for those who want to explore more on the subject. But whatever resource you choose, make sure that, in the end, your beliefs line up with the Bible. That, of course, is the most important and authoritative book of all. And even then, as you put your beliefs into practice, recognize that it doesn't mean we'll all agree.

With that said, it's my prayer that the book you're holding right now will encourage clergywomen and help educate the men who work with them about some of the issues we face. It's not all bad, believe me; and I have many wonderful, sacred stories about ministry to tell as well. But the reality is that there are things that happen to us as females – circumstances and attitudes that we face – that our male counterparts will never know about if we don't discuss them or promote dialogue about them.

To enhance our working relationships, we all need to be more educated about the differing views on women, particularly in pastoral positions, and how to handle contradictory opinions with wisdom and grace.

I suppose I've always done my share of crying, especially when there's no other way to contain my feelings. I know that men ain't supposed to cry, but I think that's wrong. Crying's always been a way for me to get things out which are buried deep, deep down. When I sing, I often cry. Crying is feeling, and feeling is being human. Oh yes, I cry.

- *Ray Charles*

CHAPTER 9

TRAFFIC JAMS

Crybaby.

It's a term I love to hate.

As a little girl, tears came easily to me. And my mother reinforced my crying by telling me she'd named me after my cousin Shirley, who I was "just like." She cried at the drop of a hat too.

As a child, it didn't compute whether that was a good or bad thing, or just something Mom liked to say. But I knew from a young age that my tears caused her distress on some level. Even though the first thing we expect a baby to do naturally after leaving the womb is cry, the direct and indirect messages I received growing up about the act turned my tears into a source of embarrassment early on in life.

Even my children used to make fun of me for this tendency during sappy movies. They would all turn around and, in unison, say, "Mommy's crying again."

Now I love my children. But I didn't enjoy them making fun of an emotional reaction that came so naturally. What's wrong with a few happy, sappy tears anyway? It was reminiscent of my mother making a big deal of my crying; and it reinforced the idea that, perhaps, there was something wrong with my behavior.

But is there?

As an adult, I've been told both, "God's given you those tears. You should rejoice over them!" and the completely contrasting, "How can you weep so easily if you're a contented Christian?" That latter stance becomes particularly problematic as a pastor. It might be nice to say that my new role made me less of a "crybaby." But that would be ignoring the realities – spiritual and otherwise – of the job.

There are many things that still trigger a misty-eyed reaction in me. Beautiful symphonic music. A vibrant sunset celebrating the variegated orange and blue colors of the evening sun and sky. A bride on her wedding day. Giving and receiving unexpected gifts. Watching my children or grandchildren excel at something they love. Listening to a testimony of God's grace. Praying with someone.

These little things can easily evoke salty tears of joy and happiness.

But I've also wept other kinds of tears. Tears of hurt, anger, frustration, or of not being heard. They can come from having someone walk away and shut down communication in the middle of a disagreement, or from being unfairly reprimanded. They happen when my emotions burn so deep that crying becomes the outer response to what's happening on the inside.

Obviously, these are not happy tears. They often show up when I least expect them and, try as I might, I usually can't suppress them. So, when I'm in a work situation, the feeling that I've lost control of my emotions is actually worse than whatever is causing the crying.

Other women have told me they struggle with the same thing. We cry when we don't want to – sometimes at work in front of men. In which case, the reactions we get are varied, from outright disgust to that caught-in-the-headlights look that says, "I have no idea what you expect me to do right now."

Executive coach Scott Cronin is quoted as saying with some exaggeration, "A woman crying at work is more threatening for a man than having someone pull a knife on him." He says that crying instantly ends a conversation. "When a woman cries, men feel confused. Their natural instinct is either avoidance or impulsively suggesting a solution to whatever provoked the situation. Men (and actually many women too) want to do or say *anything* to fill the space while someone else cries." [1]

Now, some people aren't wired to be very emotional, at least in an outward way. But my calling has allowed plenty of opportunity to experience inner emotional turmoil: the kind that simply comes with the responsibility of taking care of God's call to the people I serve.

Pastors, both male and female, are often the keepers of people's deepest secrets and thoughts. And we're called on to help others through the best and darkest of times.

We grieve with families during times of loss. We celebrate with them during marriages and births. And that joy or sorrow is then mixed with the responsibilities of performing the rituals and services to meet these needs. On top of that, we're burdened for the lost and for those who have the potential to know God on a deeper level yet seem to have little interest in doing so. Sometimes we even weep over those people who have been in the church so long yet still don't seem any more Christian in their behavior than they were 10 years ago.

We fellowship and eat meals at our church members' homes. We worship and celebrate communion. We laugh with and otherwise emotionally engage with our congregation. Because that's what we're supposed to do: what we were called to do.

I believe the emotional state of a church is only as healthy as the people who attend; and the pastor is exposed to more of its fluctuations than anyone else involved. He or she is, by default, the model of emotional health for others – a fact that has significant implications. I've been concerned at times that some of my male counterparts don't always acknowledge this and either deny or bury their emotions or, at the least, are not in touch with their feelings in an occupation that's often filled with them.

If it's not someone else's burdens we're engaging with, it's our own.

There are many helpful resources I've come across that have helped me see myself and my emotions in a more healthy light. For example, a few years ago, I read a book by Anne Kreamer called *It's Always Personal: Emotion in the New Workplace,*[2] which is a great resource to top off the other books and programs listed in these pages. Kreamer's work further enhanced my understanding of female emotions and the core from which they evolve, exploring why workplace displays of emotion are often seen as shameful. She also delves into how the different emotional rules are applied to men and women, and how those affect our modern notions of gender equality.

Specifically, Kreamer offers the results of her research about six emotional "flashpoints" – anger, fear, anxiety, empathy, joy and crying – and how they're rooted in neurological foundations. While I understood that all of those feelings existed in some way or another, her discussion of that last flashpoint really resonated with the "crybaby" moments in my life. She states that:

> Women... produce higher levels of prolactin, the hormone that controls tears, which means that generally women are, in fact, hardwired to cry more frequently. So yes, women do cry more than men, but it's not because we're weaker or less rational; it's how we're built.[3]

She cites neurologist William Frey, who states that, in general, women cry almost four times as often as men.[4] And because of how cortisol – a hormone released during stressful situations – functions in the brain, *we can't decide not to.* Cortisol automatically triggers responses such as tears, particularly in women. In other words, tears just come. Then we have to deal with the results.

Learning all of that was a very freeing concept. How many times had I sternly told myself, "You will not cry!" only to find my cheeks wet anyway? It never occurred to me that chemicals in my brain controlled those tears! Now that I'm aware of these internal physical and psychological workings, it's information I wish I could share with every man who works with women. We're genuinely not trying to make them feel awkward by letting our emotions escape this way. Believe me... We feel awkward about it too.

I once worked in a corporate position where my boss, a real humdinger, would actually revel in making me cry. Simply stated, he was a bully. I would try so hard to prepare for any interaction with him because it was almost always negative. But most times, tears would come anyway out of sheer frustration and anger at not being able to get along. Although my inability to control my physical reaction with this person caused me great emotional distress back then, it later served as a powerful learning experience on how to recognize and deal with such responses.

Most men, of course, aren't like that old boss of mine. They don't like to see obvious signs of people being hurt, particularly women. Supporting Cronin's previously mentioned assessment that men prefer knife attacks to feminine tears, Kreamer quotes Penn State psychologist Stephanie Shields, who says that women crying at work evokes "brain pain" for men.[5] They may feel confused or helpless and want to avoid or fix it for us.

This helped me understand what some of my male colleagues might be feeling when a woman cries on the job. It also helped me see how this is an issue neither men nor women should simply sweep under the rug.

Pastor, professor and author Mary Rearick Paul covered that same topic when she wrote:

> One friend of mine expressed his surprise at the amount of emotional distress some new women staff members brought to their staff meetings. He was completely baffled by the shedding of tears and expressions of hurt during these gatherings. This was not something he wanted to handle in the workplace. The uncomfortable meetings were indicators that, as the leader, he might need to explore some new approaches to decision-making and collaboration. These meetings were also a signal that these women might need to find new ways of expressing concerns and entering into leadership challenges.[6]

This is a good observation that expresses the need for personal and professional growth as coworkers. And when the tears are genuine, unintentional and unexpected, I propose that male leaders recognize the fact that their female colleagues or employees might not be able to hold them back... or even that they might have a good reason for them.

As I stated before, while our tears might make men uncomfortable, we may feel even worse about them. Many women have been told all their lives that this behavior is unacceptable, and so they may feel stupid or angry in the moment and after. It can be downright embarrassing – even humiliating – depending on who we're with at the time. Like that old boss of mine.

But while this definitely presents a problem, men really don't have to fix it any more than they should avoid it. If you are a male leader working with a female who is crying, perhaps you could just give her a minute to collect herself?

And don't hesitate to dialogue with her about it at some point, perhaps asking what the tears were about or explaining how you were affected by them. This is better than getting upset yourself or leaving the room.

U.S. Naval Academy Professors Brad Johnson and David Smith offer powerful words of advice specifically directed to male mentors of women leaders in their book entitled *Athena Rising: How and Why Men Should Mentor Women*:

> On the whole, women are freer with tears than men. So gentlemen, as a mentor for women, here is your challenge: if and when she cries, don't freak out! Her tears are not a sign of weakness, incompetence, or fragility. Tears are not inconsistent with excellent work, including first-rate leadership. If your female mentee tends to cry more than you do, if tears help her express frustration, anger, or self-doubt, then keep a box of Kleenex handy, be empathetic, and don't dare allow a few tears to diminish your regard for her.[7]

And to women, Kreamer offers this corresponding insight:

> Each of us needs to understand that tears communicate the fact that something in our lives is out of kilter right now: We are overworked, we are sick, we feel taken advantage of, we are angry, we are frustrated. *But we are*

not weak people or failures. What matters is that we step back, rationally, without undue judgment, and figure out what is going on. Don't ignore the tears. Use the occasion of crying to analyze and assess.[8]

This advice for both male and female leaders supports strategies that advance emotional intelligence, a topic we'll discuss further in the next chapter. In the meantime, it's important to understand what's might be causing tears in the first place. Because, in line with Kreamer's six flashpoints, episodes of crying can also be sparked by another key emotion – anger.

As I contemplated the situations in ministry that have made me most angry, the No. 1 culprits are without a doubt not being heard and/or being misheard. So many times, men in particular have repeated what they thought I said in a meeting, yet it wasn't what I meant at all.

Now, misunderstandings do happen sometimes. To some degree, they're even unavoidable when each one of us operates out of our own perspective, shaped by our upbringing, personalities, strengths, weaknesses, statuses, experiences and, yes, genders. However, there have been repeated times when I've tried to clarify, only to be summarily shut down.

At one point, I even stopped sharing publicly in pastor's meetings because it seemed that whatever I said was almost always misunderstood. Perhaps worse yet were the times when, a few minutes after I'd raised an idea and it was ignored or rejected, a man would say the same thing, only for everyone to immediately get it, enact it and applaud the contribution. Nor is this experience specific to me, since other female leaders both inside and outside of the church have related similar occurrences.

That's worth some righteous anger – maybe even some angry tears – provided that we keep it righteous.

Personally, I've found it difficult to express anger during a meeting, even a one-on-one, while on the verge of tears. There's a sense of vulnerability – especially the loss of what I consider my professional decorum. When that happens, it intensifies my emotions and usually tears of frustration spill out – like it or not.

I've also been in situations where men have appropriately voiced anger, and their feelings were acknowledged, and even accepted. But if, in a similar way, a woman vents anger, especially while displaying tears, she stands to lose collegial respect, and may even take a hit to perceptions about her integrity. So sometimes, a woman feels caught in a lose-lose situation, and will remain quiet, preferring to keep the tears at bay rather than risk being open and vulnerable.

It's also been my experience that anger can be an especially dangerous emotion to show around church people. Some view any form of it as a sign of unrighteousness or lack of control even though Jesus himself displayed righteous anger toward the Pharisees and even his own disciples at times.

The Apostle Paul also spoke about anger in Ephesians 4:26-27: "In your anger do not sin: Do not let the sun go down while you are still angry, and do not give the devil a foothold." Here, he addresses anger as a normal part of human emotion, as do many other New and Old Testament passages. So, we see that the emotion of anger is not our problem; it's what we do with anger when it comes to the surface, is harbored inside, or ignored altogether.

Clearly, it's inappropriate to go around screaming our heads off at people. But it's normal to become genuinely angry now and then at a person or situation. Or even ourselves. And anger must be managed.

Sometimes I get mad at myself because I didn't handle something or someone well. Other times, I've gotten angry when somebody has caused hurt to me or someone else. Truth be told, on a day-to-day basis, we humans are probably going to face a variety of things that make us angry. And as pastors, we also have to help other people when they experience such strong emotions too.

For instance, I once worked with a woman who was a wonderfully supportive laywoman. One day, she came to me after church, visibly upset because another female congregant had dumped on her that morning. The second woman was mad because the church ladies' group had decided not to host a baby shower for one of her relatives. I vividly recall standing in my office with this beautiful laywoman who was on the verge of frustrated tears, angry with me because I wasn't going to do anything about the situation.

Understanding her emotional reaction, I gently responded with, "Look. You're standing here so upset. And you want me to be upset too. But the lady who dumped on you is home right now enjoying lunch. Don't you think there's something wrong with this picture?"

She got it then, understanding how it was the angry woman's responsibility to come to me instead of using someone else as a pawn between us. And yes, that kind of intentional manipulation made me angry too. Incidentally, we never did hold that baby shower.

Tales of righteously angry people can be found throughout Scripture, featuring Moses, David, Samuel – even God! The Bible makes it clear that we are, in fact, allowed to be angry. And, since God literally designed women to cry – and men too, even if to a lesser extent – we're allowed to tear up when we feel as if we can't do anything constructive with that anger.

And think of this: the tendency to cry or be angry opens the door to yet another aspect of life where we can learn to give ourselves grace and love... even during times when our emotions surface more easily than others.

And, let's face it. Sometimes the things we get mad over aren't worth the effort anyway.

For those times when it is, I have realized this: I would much rather express my emotions through crying and feel embarrassed for a moment than to say things that hurt someone. That's a personal conviction made even stronger by my vocation. I think it goes without saying that being careful to not wound others should hold true for pastors across the board, men or women.

If dealing with all this sounds virtually impossible, there is help available. Some situations or periods in life may even call for professional Christian counseling. For pastors in particular, there are actually counselors out there who work primarily with us and understand the demands of the life we lead. This is something I've utilized myself during periods of great stress, especially during big life transitions like changing jobs or moving from one church to another. It was beneficial to have an unbiased person listen to what I was feeling and guide me in how to handle my stress levels: tears, anger and all.

But that's not the end of the journey to well-being. Not even close…

> Loving ourselves through
> the process of owning our story
> is the bravest thing we will ever do.
>
> *- Brené Brown*

CHAPTER 10

KNOW WHO'S DRIVING

Let's face it,… nobody's perfect.

So why do so many women strive to be?

One of my favorite authors is professor and vulnerability researcher Dr. Brené Brown, who encourages her readers to get real about who we are and to embrace ways to share our authentic selves with others – to really see our gifts and talents, and to accept our imperfections.

But not everyone pays attention to this kind of thing.

Imagine someone who really doesn't know himself or herself that well: someone who instead lives in a self-image framework that other people have painted for them. "You're this or you're that," others say. And this person believes it, whether it's true or not.

Now put that idea into the context of the Scripture we first brought up in Chapter 7: what Jesus himself calls the most important commandments in Matthew 22:37-40:

> … 'Love the Lord your God with all your heart, and with all your soul and with all your mind.' This is the first and greatest commandment. And the second is like it: 'Love your neighbor *as yourself*" [emphasis mine].

We are reminded again by Jesus' words here that establishing proper self-love is a core component to loving others. And the entirety of all love – in heart, soul, mind and spirit – is sourced by and in the Lord.

But if we are to truly love ourselves as Jesus states here, then how do we go about discovering who we really are in Christ? In what way has the Lord created each of us as unique human beings? How can we become more self-aware, understanding what makes us tick so we can better love the Lord and serve Him by loving others?

No doubt, reading or listening to Scripture and praying for insight can reveal much to us. We can be affirmed of our positive attributes as well as challenged to grow. And we can be set free from any false images instilled in us to discover the true image of Christ as intended when we were knit together in our mother's womb. Whatever the Lord shows us, it takes courage to face our true selves and keep moving more deeply into the likeness of Christ.

In one of her earliest books, *I Thought I Was Just Me: Women Reclaiming Power and Courage in a Culture of Shame*, Brené writes:

> Courage is a heart word. The root of the word courage is cor – the Latin word for heart. In one of its earliest forms, the word courage meant "To speak one's mind by telling all one's heart." Over time, this definition has changed, and today, we typically associate courage with heroic and brave deeds. But in my opinion, this definition fails to recognize the inner strength and level of commitment required for us to actually speak honestly and openly about who we are and about our experiences – good and bad. Speaking from our hearts is what I think of as "ordinary courage."[1]

I sometimes play with a mental image of a world full of people who really like themselves and who truly accept who they are without apology. People who have escaped the bondage of perfectionism and live authentically. People who can see themselves through the loving, compassionate eyes of Christ.

What a world that would be!

I have a deep desire to see myself as Christ sees me. To love myself as he instructs. To put aside forever the things I've been told – even the things I've told myself – about who I am. As I set out on this road of self-discovery, endeavoring to unearth who I am in God's image, there is no doubt that Scripture has given me the most insight.

But there are also other helpful tools that have aided my progress towards self-awareness.

I share a few here in hopes that they will assist others in the same manner.

The first of these is the emotional intelligence profile (known as EQ). Completing the EQ inventory, and expanding on it with subsequent training, has helped me identify my emotional states and learn how to manage them better. This includes the effects I might have on someone else or how others may respond to me when we interact together.

As a science journalist, psychologist Dr. Daniel Goleman reported for many years on the brain and behavioral sciences for The New York Times. In 1995, he penned the book *Emotional Intelligence: Why It Can Matter More Than IQ*. The keystone of EQ, he says, is "awareness of one's own feelings as they occur."[2]

Goleman contends that this kind of self-awareness is crucial to our well-being and social relationships. He refers to it as "self-reflexive, introspective attention to one's own experience, sometimes called *mindfulness*."[3] In other words, if we become aware of and attentive to what's happening to us emotionally on the inside, it can shape how we outwardly respond to it.

This applies to each of the four tenets of EQ. Two are listed as personal competencies: self-awareness and self-management. And two are social competencies: social awareness and relationship management, both of which involve how we relate to others.

In an article posted on his website on March 8, 2016, Goleman writes, complete with bold text:

> The most effective leaders, we've long known, have more competence in emotional intelligence. **It's not your college degrees or IQ that make you an outstanding leader, but emotional intelligence abilities.** Leaders who get the best results tend to

show more strengths in key competencies in emotional intelligence.

Now the news comes that women, on average, are better at almost all these crucial leadership skills than are men on average. The two competencies where men and women had the least difference were emotional self-control and positive outlook. The largest difference was for self-awareness. [4]

He goes on to describe other areas where women on average scored better than men and says that these competencies are what leading companies look for in the people they hire, promote and groom for leadership.

> This sounds like a wake-up call to any organization: You are ignoring a critical factor in your own success if you lag in recruiting women to leadership positions – and most companies are in that boat.

And he continues with:

> ... just as companies need to avoid a bias favoring men for leadership positions, the answer does not lie in an across-the-board bias favoring women instead. **The smart way to use this finding lies in spotting the RIGHT women for leadership.**[5]

Goleman's work has since been enhanced by Travis Bradberry and Jean Greaves in their book, "Emotional Intelligence 2.0"[6] As such, taking the EQ online profile is only the beginning of how this body of work can help. By studying and applying the strategies offered in a personal assessment, we can better see how our emotional state functions in our relationships with others. This information can then offer concrete ways to improve as a person and a pastor.

I've seen it firsthand.

One way EQ helped me in ministry was in discovering that, although my personal competencies were strong (i.e., I know myself pretty well), I had a lower score in social competencies. This enlightened me to ways I could intentionally improve how other people received me.

For example, I examined how well I communicate, something I think I'm pretty good at. Having been a communications skills trainer in the past, my working definition of effective communication is "a two-way dialogue in which the message is sent, received and understood as intended by the sender." Thus, when interacting with congregants, the church board or committees – even in my preaching – I became more cognizant of how I came across to people. Did they receive the message I intended to send?

It's amazing how our words and actions can affect people, even when we mean absolutely no harm or are perhaps trying to be funny. While this applies to both men and women, pastors or otherwise, a few situations I've personally experienced automatically come to mind – times when a leader's social intelligence could improve how they communicate and thus, how they're received by others.

Have you ever sat listening to a speaker who has obviously lost the attention of their audience, but they don't seem to realize it? They go on and on... and on. In that case, this person may lack the social intelligence capacity to recognize their audience's emotional state.

Another example comes from a purely biological perspective. There are things that women experience like menstruation or menopause that men don't have to deal with. We can be the butt of jokes about how "hormonal" we are or how flushed our faces get during a hot flash. And women who are breastfeeding have to carefully plan things out even more. To complicate matters further, as pastors, we're required to lead a complete worship service or chair a meeting as if nothing is happening.

This is no laughing matter.

I've been at activities where the male leader, with no ill intention whatsoever, has thoughtlessly said something like, "Well, we're going to pray in a few minutes and I ask that no one leave the room now."

Well, a woman who is menstruating may not be able to wait. For that matter, neither can a parent with a crying baby. Or someone who isn't feeling well. Yet anyone who might genuinely need to leave is automatically going to feel very conspicuous – like everyone is watching them pick up their purse or baby or self and walk out.

All of us, male and female, can develop greater sensitivity to situations like these by becoming conscious of who's in the room and how our bodies might be working differently. That's a form of social intelligence in action.

Of course, effective communication gets disrupted all the time. Sometimes it's our fault; sometimes it's someone else's. Either way, it can be frustrating. Recognizing that, I began to employ two social intelligence strategies: 1) Watch for body language and 2) Actively listen. I purposefully practiced using more clarifying questions and paraphrases to get feedback so I could know if my message came across properly.

Were just my emotions showing? Just my logic? Or were the two working hand in hand together? It's like that saying: "I know you believe you understand what you think I said, but I'm not sure you realize that what you heard is not what I meant."[7]

Truth is, we can all develop greater sensitivity to our differences and similarities, asking ourselves if we're being received the way we think we are. And a second key component to achieving that lies in the discovery of our personality temperaments.

Years ago, before the concept of emotional intelligence became so popular, I was hired to consult with a business that sold industrial safety equipment. My task was to provide training for the representatives, complete with a "sales university" that outlined a comprehensive one-year training process. Part of that included establishing core competencies in each skill area and determining what tools to use to achieve the desired results.

In addition, the company wanted to incorporate some type of personality assessment to help its sales representatives better understand themselves and their customers. And so they sent me to California to get certified in personality profiles with Florence Littauer.

Not only did I come back ready to train the sales and customer services representatives; I also returned with a lot more knowledge about my own dominant personality temperament and what makes me tick. It has been a valuable resource ever since.

Admitting this and studying up on it has led to some truly wonderful breakthroughs in my church experience. Being able to quickly recognize a person's dominant personality attributes and temperament has provided a key filter for how I see myself and those I interact with. I can now quickly spot the person who is choleric (dominant extrovert), like me, enjoys being the leader and works best when things are under control.

I've placed melancholy (perfectionist introverts) personalities in key roles like treasurer and administrative assistant. Since their attention to detail is top-notch, they'll automatically notice things I would otherwise miss. I've hired sanguine types (socially engaging extroverts) whose desire for fun can provide a much-needed balance to my serious side. And then there are those wonderful phlegmatics (stability-seeking introverts), who take things in stride and provide peace and calm in many a board meeting.

Knowing my temperament, combined with the tenets of EQ, has really helped me get in touch with what makes me angry, happy, sad and so on. I've learned to do better handling my own emotions, simultaneously recognizing that, in any given situation, others may not perceive me the same way I'm perceiving myself.

Overall, it's remarkably liberating to have enough self-awareness that, even when others don't understand what I'm trying to convey, I GET ME. And that really can make a world of difference. It gives me peace and encourages me to keep loving myself even though it might feel like someone else hasn't understood or even rejected me or what I have to say.

The idea here is to be healthy about self-reflection, not self-centered or to try to become perfect. Again, quoting from Brené Brown:

> Healthy striving is self-focused: "How can I improve?"
> Perfectionism is other-focused: "What will they think?" [8]

We can easily get caught up worrying about what other people think of us rather than focusing on who God made us to be and celebrating our irreplaceable individuality.

One final resource along those lines that I highly recommend is the StrengthsFinder profile, which intentionally only reveals each test-taker's top five strengths out of a possible thirty-four.[9] The idea is to focus on what you're naturally strong at rather than trying to improve on your weaknesses, which was the traditional way of thinking. For me, it's rounded out my understanding of my gifts as revealed by traditional spiritual gifts profiles I've taken in the past, helping me see how to identify and operate in the areas of my strengths and gifts even more closely.

Awareness of dominant strengths is especially beneficial for most pastors since most of us have to wear so many hats. The plates are always spinning, and there is always something or someone to attend to in the church. So understanding what we are naturally good at can really help us focus on where we can make the greatest impact – and become better at delegating tasks to others who have strengths we don't have. There are just some things we are not naturally wired to do and be.

As an example, I know that I am not particularly good at pastoral visitation at the hospital. That doesn't mean I can't or won't do it. It's considered part of the job description. But it's been freeing to learn that this aspect of ministry will never come naturally to me – that I don't have to add one more pressure on myself to make it come naturally. I marvel at people who can walk into a hospital room and instantly create an atmosphere of peace and calm. They know exactly what to say to comfort the patient.

For me though, it's a part of my role that's always been awkward. And I have to wonder whether truly sick or suffering people want to be made even more uncomfortable by being visited by someone who doesn't know what to say or how to say it in such circumstances.

I can assure you that any suitable statements I do make are given by the grace of God alone!

Because of how my strengths play out, I would much rather work with someone on a strategic plan. I know - a pastor isn't supposed to admit such a thing. We're supposed to exude absolute willingness in every aspect of our ministries. Besides, the automatic expectation is that it's our job – not to mention a woman's role – to make people feel encouraged and assisted in the hospital room or nursing home.

But what comes naturally to some is not true for all of us. Fortunately, there are others who have strengths in the areas I'm weak. That's how the body of Christ works.

God didn't make a single one of us perfect any more than he made us imperfect. Not even when we're called to be pastors. While everyone is good at something, we're also all not so good at other things. For me, learning what those things are has been a critical component of learning to love myself as God created me to be.

For example, merging what I learned about my top five strengths with discoveries from the EQ assessment equipped me to see how my emotions are affected when I'm required to perform duties that take me away from my strengths and into areas of weakness. I've learned to stay focused on my areas of strength and not apologize for the parts of pastoral ministry I'm not strong in. I've been able to practice patience and compassion with myself for the functions of ministry that I'm not the best at, while celebrating how God uses my particular strengths, and those of others, to advance the kingdom.

The good news is that God has given each of us talents to use for Him and others. That's why we're called the body of Christ, and it's a beautiful thing! While some people are good at planning, others are good at executing. While some prefer tasks, others prefer people. I've been fortunate to have individuals around me with other strengths that compliment mine. These are the folks I identify to delegate aspects of ministry that allow them to operate in their strengths, which results in joy for everyone involved and brings glory to God.

The diagnostic tools I've presented here are useful for everyone, and I highly recommend using them no matter your occupation. They can help you discover who you are and how you're wired. And whatever the results, you can then submit them to the leadership of the Holy Spirit. Let him do the work in you that will help you love yourself and others with holy love, becoming all you can be in Christ in the process.

> ...I can no longer pretend
> like I have it all together
> ... I am broken too.
>
> *Pastor Stephanie Dryness Lobdell*
> *from "Pastors and Mental Illness"*
> *Blog post: August 28, 2018*
> *www.stephanielobdell.com*

CHAPTER 11

RUNNING ON EMPTY

His name is Pastor Teddy Parker, Jr.

I keep his picture on my computer desktop.

Rev. Parker, the 42-year-old pastor of the 800-member Bibb Mount Zion Baptist Church in Macon, Georgia, preached a sermon in 2010 entitled "Facing Your Storm With Confidence"[1]. In it, he encouraged his congregation by sharing, with great vulnerability, about his own struggles in his walk with God. He said:

> You know a lot of times, we feel like when we are going through stuff and it's a lot that there's nobody there with us. And guess what? God intends for you to feel that way. I know y'all been saved a long time. I know you super spiritual and you know you real holy but there are times in your life, not y'all but me. There are times in my life when I'm going through some stuff where I can't feel God there.

> I try to pray but I don't feel like God is hearing me. I try to serve but I don't feel like God is using me. And there are times in your life when God purposely withdraws from you, he doesn't withdraw for the sake of leaving you but he withdraws so you can grow and mature.

Just a few years later, on November 10, 2013, it's reported that Pastor Teddy sent his wife and two daughters to church ahead of him. His congregation was waiting for him to come and preach the sermon, but he didn't show up. His wife, Larrinecia, went home to find out what was keeping her husband. She arrived to find him in their driveway – dead from a self-inflicted gunshot wound.

You see, he suffered from manic depression (now called bipolar disorder), **but no one in church knew it**.

His longtime friend, Dr. E. Dewey Smith, Jr., senior pastor at The House of Hope Atlanta in Decatur, Georgia, said this in his eulogy: "He was suffering with manic depression, and he had some emotional issues that he had been dealing with. [He was] in treatment, but he just couldn't step away from ministry."[2]

Some pastors have been taught to never let people see that you're hurting. Although a few people close to him knew, most did not have any idea that this called man of God was struggling. Pastor Smith went on to say:

> It's hard to be honest. It's difficult for some preachers to be honest. Every pastor needs a pastor to kind of lead and guide them. But it's hard for us to really find that relationship because often pastors are trying to compete with or cremate you. And so it's difficult to find camaraderie.[3]

Congregation members described Pastor Parker as a "very caring upbeat guy that cared for people, especially with the kids" and a "good man" who inspired others and showed no signs of trouble, financially speaking or otherwise. Moreover, the church was doing well and they were in the process of building a new facility. To the people around him, including his family, everything seemed fine.

It was reported that no one saw it coming.

I didn't know Teddy Parker personally, but I grieved his death. How awful that someone who is responsible for the care of God's people is uncared for himself or herself… or that a pastor does not feel like they can be truly authentic about these things, even though they preach the same to others. This hits close to home for many I've known in ministry at times, including me.

Teddy Parker is my constant reminder
that taking care of myself in ministry
is no laughing matter.

Any clergyperson can have times when he or she is susceptible to physical, mental or emotional drain due to the constant and long hours, or ongoing conflicts in the church, or intense periods where a family needs more care, such as in the case of a loved one's death or serious illness. Clergy have been known to experience many days – even weeks – of such ministry.

It's an on-call life. Twenty-four hours a day. Seven days a week.

Pastors, regardless of the exact role they have in the church, have given their entire lives to this pursuit. It's not a job. It's a vocation. And so we remain pastors wherever we go, whether that's the supermarket, a party, a hospital or a church.

Consider the time I attended a get-together at a parishioner's home where several guests from their neighborhood were invited. During the ensuing conversation, the question came up about what our denomination believes about Jesus. And the host, a member of the church for more than 40 years, turned to me and said, "Pastor, you can answer that."

I did, but all the while wondering why he couldn't.

Another time, my husband and I went to a birthday party for his aunt who was turning 90. Mind you, this was family, not church members. In the middle of the afternoon, several of us wandered out onto the front porch to enjoy the beautiful sunny weather outside. As we talked about the struggles Ron's aunt and uncle were facing because of their age, the conversation turned to the issues of life and death.

That's when one of the younger family members turned to me – not anyone else – and said, "So where *do* we go when we die? Does our soul go straight to heaven, or is there a place in between?"

I remember thinking, "But I'm here to eat birthday cake, not have a theological conversation about where your soul goes at the end of life!"

Yet that's the situation pastors of either gender find themselves in: consistently being called on to step up to the spiritual plate. And while, for the most part, we have accepted these as opportunities and don't mind them, this way of living does have the potential to become draining. Imagine a baseball player who has to keep going up to bat even though practice is over and the game isn't until Saturday. Or an accountant who has to keep crunching numbers for friends after the normal nine-to-five shift ends. In the baseball player's case, he or she is going to become physically spent soon enough, which is bound to make them less capable of handling other areas in their life. In the accountant's, they might lose their mental edge after too long, which is bound to then affect other areas of their existence as well.

The same applies to jobs that may overload the emotions and drain the spirit.

Living with chronic stress or feeling like our tank is on empty can intensify emotional reactions and may present a challenge at times to joyfully fulfill our pastoral responsibilities. Yet like people who ask the plumber for advice at a family dinner or the doctor who's called upon to provide free diagnoses at a relative's wedding, being put on the spot like that comes with the territory for pastors. As such, we learn to adapt whether we want to or not.

This is another path that, if we ignore the road signs, can detour us into the exhaustion of physical, mental or emotional strength, or all three. After all, anyone who leads an on-call life is susceptible to burnout, a deep weariness that can occur if a person undergoes prolonged periods of stress or frustration.

I've read articles written by pastors and other Christian leaders implying that no person, especially a minister, can or will get burned out if they're in the center of God's will. The implication is that anyone who finds themselves in such an exhausted condition must be spiritually deficient: an idea I fervently oppose.

To me, this feels like a U-turn back to Old Testament times, when many illnesses were attributed to sin in a person's life or family line. Today, we have a much better understanding of issues related to mental health and wellness, and we should know that the body, mind and emotions can betray even the most spiritually minded individual.

To name this kind of fatigue as a spiritual problem is just wrong. They are separate issues, and the fact that male or female pastors may suffer from burnout does not mean they're less spiritual than those who don't – any more than a physically restricted pastor is less spiritual than a fully abled one.

Burnout can be lurking just around the bend for anyone. And clergy must learn to pay attention to themselves and the things that create overall well-being in their lives to help prevent overtiredness from blocking the road in front of us. We must value self-care as much as we value caring for others.

Admittedly, for many, this is easier said than done.

For example, like many other people, pastors or otherwise, I suffer from seasonal affective disorder, labeled appropriately as SAD. This disorder makes winter a time to be extremely alert to what's going on within my body and being. Though the specific causes of SAD remain unknown, it's believed that reduced sunlight factors in greatly. In the fall and winter, less sunshine can, therefore, cause winter-onset SAD, which disrupts the body's internal clock and can lead to feelings of depression.

Or there may be a drop in serotonin levels, a brain chemical (neurotransmitter) that affects mood and that can trigger depression. And a third possible contributor is how the change in seasons can upset the balance of the body's level of melatonin, an important dynamic in sleep patterns and mood.

The ramifications of SAD include the desire to eat more, especially carbohydrates, and to be more emotional than usual. "Winter blues" doesn't do it justice. I want to feel better, but I just don't. And because it's wrapped up in the workings of my physical body, I can't just make it go away by deciding it should.

Many years ago, my Northeast-residing husband and I began taking a Florida vacation every January so that I could be in the sun for a week or two mid-winter. This was tremendously healing for me, though it's not always an affordable option. That's why I now use a light therapy lamp on my desk that simulates sunshine without the UV rays. It helps me a lot; but for some who suffer, it may not be enough to ever feel comfortable with the winter.

As debilitating as SAD can be though, it's a small thing compared to the even more serious mental health issues that people like Pastor Teddy dealt with: depression, anxiety and other disorders that pastors can suffer from just as much as anyone else. Whatever it is we struggle with – even if it's just natural human limitations – giving ourselves permission to rest in a way that replenishes our bodies, minds, emotions and souls is also critical if we're going to sustain our vocation's demands.

Pastors get sick and have difficulties just like everyone else. We are not immune. I know pastors who have cancer, whose family members have passed away, who have suffered from depression and other mental health challenges, whose finances are so, so tight - and the list goes on. We grieve and hurt just like the people we care for in ministry. And sometimes, it can feel overwhelming as Pastor Teddy expressed.

There can be loneliness in ministry even when we're in a crowd. And there can be outside pressure just because life happens.

During the course of my most recent, nine-year pastoral assignment, my brother Marvin became very ill and was hospitalized about three hours away from where I lived. Some of his other family members called me, as they weren't sure what to do.

My brother had multiple myeloma, sleep apnea and a heart condition. The story is too long, detailed and personal to share here, but the point is that while someone else aided him with his physical health, I took care of his financial and legal affairs for over two years. This included helping him relocate, and I handled the sale of his house, which was three hours away from where I lived. This process included working with engineers, plumbers and contractors over a period of many months to get things up to code.

Additionally, his home was burglarized after we moved his belongings, and it was a very stressful couple of years as I juggled these responsibilities and the emotions that went with them in addition to my regular work as a church pastor.

Then, in 2015, after over 20 years of full-time ministry, I took my first-ever sabbatical leave. It was wonderful! A blissful seven weeks to step away, rest and regroup. I was drained in every regard and really in need of the break.

Then, in the last week of my time away, I received a phone call that Marvin had been rushed to the hospital – and that he didn't make it. He died in the ambulance on the way there.

So, on my first day back from sabbatical, I was busy visiting the undertaker with my other brother and various family members. A few days later, on a cold February morning, we held Marvin's funeral. Then I was right back into the ministerial thick of things, only now I was also in a state of deep grief.

During that same time period of time, my husband's brother was dying of cancer. Since his brother lived alone and needed a caregiver, Ron had been staying with him much of the time, taking him to chemotherapy treatments and many other doctor's visits. So, Ron and I were apart much of the time for over two years, including the months after my brother passed away.

And it didn't get any easier from there. Not for a while longer.

Just a few months later, in May, our oldest son became very ill very suddenly, having seizures and other physical difficulties. A normally healthy man, the doctors could not figure out what was causing his problems. He was hospitalized for many weeks and for most of that time, kept in an induced coma to keep him calm.

We thought he was going to die several times, and it was one of the most agonizing experiences I've ever had as we watched our child suffer, powerless to do anything to help him.

Thankfully, Pastor Gates helped our church family out as they watched us grieve. He even came on a Sunday morning and led the congregation to pray for us and our family, inviting them to share in the experience with us.

Ron and I were both emotionally and physically exhausted from wondering what would happen to our first-born son. I knew from what happened to Pastor Gates and Judy's daughter, Heather, that being a Christian doesn't keep sickness and problems away. I knew that not everybody's child makes it through. Some pass away.

Thankfully, our son did not, and he eventually recuperated – a true miracle.

But then in July, Ron's brother passed away, leaving Ron to take care of packing up things in his home for his niece, who worked full time and lived several states away. He disposed of many things and refurbished several rooms. And we grieved some more.

It was a very emotional season for both of us. By August, my sabbatical leave felt like it had never happened.

And I thought of Pastor Teddy Parker often during that period, including when I decided to talk with my church board to say, "I'm grieving. And I'm screwing up in the process. Will you be patient with me while I grieve?"

I realized the importance of having others know what was going on, and to help hold me up in the process. Yet I admit that I considered whether admitting my needs would make me seem weak as a leader, especially as a female leader.

Of course, lots of people, in pastoral ministry or not, go through situations like mine. As clergy, I've had the privilege of walking alongside them when things are tough. As mentioned earlier, pastors pray with families, help people grieve, visit them in hospitals, and try to focus on helping them look to the Lord and take care of their own spiritual needs. But like any person involved in care giving, when the same things you are helping people through are also happening to you, it feels doubly stressful.

Because of seasons like this, I've learned that – yes, I'll say it again – we pastors must pay attention to our own well-being and practice self-care. We cannot – must not – rely on others to do this for us. Otherwise, we can run the risk of contracting compassion fatigue. We should not ignore the fact that the extreme tension and preoccupation with helping others who are suffering can create a secondary traumatic stress for the helper.

Any caregiver can become depleted physically, mentally, emotionally and spiritually. And it's true: no person can give out what they don't have. We need health and spiritual vitality to stay in love with what we do each day. We need to be connected with the source of our spiritual energy.

I am so thankful that the Lord modeled ways to protect us from the exhaustion that life can bring.

Like Jesus, we can retreat from people at times.

Like Jesus, we must rest.

And, like Jesus, we can make our connection to the Father our No. 1 priority.

By the seventh day God had finished the work he had been doing; so on the seventh day he rested from all his work. Then God blessed the seventh day and made it holy, because on it he rested from all the work of creating that he had done.

Genesis 2:2-3

CHAPTER 12

REST STOPS

"Are you taking *another* vacation?"

It's surprised me how many times I've been asked this question - not by members of my congregation, but by other pastors! It's not like I take that many. Yet to some clergymen and women, even one annual getaway is too much.

For many years, I participated as a staff member during an annual assessment weekend for new clergy preparing for ordination. And every year, without fail, the participants were cautioned to learn quickly to schedule time off on a regular basis in order to rest and refresh. That might include a hike in the woods, a day at the beach, fishing or fun with the family.

Most seasoned pastors agree there must be a routine "off" switch, whether that's with a date night, a personal retreat day, a vacation or sabbatical, or intentional physical activity and exercise. But just imagine how challenging this can be when a person is a co-vocational minister who already juggles two schedules for work. Or how about parents whose children are young, or those who are caregivers to a spouse, adult child, or aging parent? Or what about the person who doesn't have available vacation time from work nor the money to afford to go away somewhere?

In all of those cases and many more like them, planned rest breaks can quickly lose priority amidst other daily needs.

Yes, pastoral work is known as a high-stress vocation. Just ask any insurance company about the cost of group health insurance and where pastors fall on the list to learn how true that is. A lot is expected. A recent article I read hit the mark:

It seems we should suggest to our young ministerial students that pursuing a degree in five or six subjects might be what they will need. We could probably all come up with a list that includes business administration, finance, psychology, sociology, education, communication, and marketing, along with theology, philosophy, biblical studies, church history, and more.[1]

Thus, the nature of this vocation compels us to learn various ways to disconnect if we are to remain healthy. "Downtime" is a crucial component to overall well-being and making sure we don't let it get away from us is vital. Yes, many things can get in the way of clergy self-care. Even pre-planned times of rest can be unexpectedly interrupted, like needing to perform a funeral service during scheduled time off for vacation. After all, we can't schedule death.

Yet we know that Sabbath rest is modeled in the creation story – in the beginning. Even God took a break to stop, rest and enjoy it all.

In my denomination, the amount of time we earn for vacation is tied to the number of years we're in full-time ministry. Starting out, I received one week per year. After 20 years, I was eligible for five. Yet neither option makes scheduling vacation necessarily easy. There are just too many factors to consider.

When I served at a smaller church, for instance, I often planned my time away so that I would not be gone on a Sunday, especially when we didn't have an associate pastor to fill the pulpit. Otherwise, it would have cost the church to pay someone to come and preach in my place. I was also taught to be careful how many Sundays I was away each year. Thus, even the five-week option often meant leaving after church Sunday and returning the next Saturday to avoid missing too many services.

Indeed, I've known a few pastors who never feel like they can ever be away on a Sunday morning. And while I respect each person's ability to decide what's best for their situation, I've always believed that if the church or ministry you're in charge of can't run without you for a while, something just might be wrong. We have to learn to delegate and trust others, even when we know things might not get done the way we would do them.

According to the Bible, members of the congregation have been gifted by God to serve their part. It's important to give space for that to happen even when we're present. But vacation or sabbatical time both offer a unique opportunity to let go and let God's people handle things.

Having said that, I do agree that choosing the right person to preach in a pastor's absence deserves special consideration. Whether it's a layperson or clergy, it's not just a matter of having a warm body to stand in the pulpit. Especially in the case of an extended absence, like sabbatical leave, the person addressing the congregation can either usher in peace and joy, or chaos and problems. So choose carefully.

Believe me, I've seen it backfire badly. This may factor into why some pastors don't like to step away at all. Even so, stepping away is essential for everybody – pastor and people.

Likewise, it's imperative that we pastors set healthy boundaries, first with ourselves and then with others. This is especially necessary for our families' sakes. Otherwise, it's easy to rob them of our presence by being distracted or flat-out interrupted by matters that can actually wait.

Along those lines, it's valuable to consider taking breaks away from technology too. Some scheduled-in distance from cell phones, text messages and emails in addition to actual meetings and discussions, can help foster the rest we need, including better-quality sleep at night.

In my role as pastor, I usually have lots of physical stamina and don't tire easily. But my emotional state and mental freshness is another thing. And a contributing factor, one that affects millions of people, is the overwhelming tendency in America to not get enough sleep.

Studies have linked sleep deprivation to all kinds of problems, including physical ailments, accidents on the highway, and loss of business income due to poor productivity.

For me, losing sleep happens for a variety of reasons. I've often woken up in the middle of the night with thoughts for the basis of my weekly sermon. As nice as it would be to wait until morning to write them down, I've learned to get up and capture them when they come. They slip away too easily if I don't.

Going to bed after a board meeting or while conflicts are brewing can also mean a restless night's sleep. So can anticipating a major upcoming event, like a trip, conference or vacation. And think of the challenge of developing and maintaining proper sleep habits for a co-vocational pastor who may work odd shifts or late into the night! Or the one with an infant who wakes up many times before the sun comes up?

These kinds of issues are common to lots of people I know, pastor or not. But because pastors are on call most hours even when we're not at church, it can lead to even higher stress levels. That's why it's so important to understand your exact situation and needs, not to mention your exact tendencies and reactions, both physical and emotional.

I know that when Ron was away caring for his brother and I was alone many evenings, I would often turn on the television, if only for background noise. But then, if I did get caught up in a show, I would stay up too late and be tired the next day. As such, I no longer have a television in the bedroom, so I can no longer climb into bed thinking "I'll just watch the news for a minute".

Additionally, if I consume caffeine after five o'clock, I know without a doubt that sleep will be hard to find when I go to bed later. Some people don't struggle with this at all, but when it's your reality, it's wise to pay attention to it. Because I also know for sure that, when I'm not properly rested, I am more irritable and less able to focus on the details of the day.

And studies have shown that women have some unique sleep characteristics to consider. There are distinct differences between how men and women sleep, the amount of sleep they require, and the challenges they face to get to sleep and stay asleep.

In an online article, "Do Women Need More Sleep Than Men?", Britain's leading sleep science expert, Dr. Jim Horne, says the answer is yes. Several factors that may affect women's quantity and quality of sleep are:

- Sleep disturbances during pregnancy due to excess weight and position of the fetus.

- Difficulty sleeping during menopause due to hot flashes.

- Being woken up and moved around on the bed by the partner. (Men tend to be larger than women)

- Worrying about problems and losing sleep as a result.[2]

Additional gender-specific discrepancies are listed by **www.sleep.org** in a web post, "The Difference Between a Man & Woman's Sleep":

- Women require about 20 more minutes of sleep than men do. That's because they expend more mental energy each day – in other words, they multitask and use more of their brains. Sleep is the time when the brain regenerates, and since women's brains have more work to do during slumber, they require more of it.

- Women experience more sleep troubles. While men are more prone to sleep apnea, women suffer from insomnia two to three times more often. About 15 percent of women report having sleep troubles, versus only eight percent of men. (Unfortunately, when women pass menopause, their likelihood of developing sleep apnea is about equal to that of men).

- Women don't handle sleep deprivation well. Women have a tougher time with inadequate shut-eye. Compared with men, women are impacted more by sleep deprivation, especially when it comes to their mental state. They report more anger, depression, and hostility than men when they don't get enough sleep. Insufficient slumber can also increase the risk of diabetes and cardiovascular disease for both men and women.

Overall, both the quantity and quality of sleep are important to anyone's overall well-being, regardless of their gender or professional role. And the lack thereof directly impacts performance and cognitive ability in general. Sleeping enough hours each night and getting into REM sleep helps every intertwined aspect of our being: physical, mental, emotional and spiritual. And when one aspect doesn't get the proper attention it needs, it can very easily upset the others.

Depending on our individual composition, strengths, weaknesses and situations, the effects of this imbalance can show up in different ways.

Maybe like crying. Or being cranky.

Or any one of the other physical issues that can pile up and impact a person's health.

Whatever your body's outlet is, don't ignore it no matter your circumstance. Today, just the sheer speed of life and technology can create an underlying, persistent pressure that creeps up on us. We automatically adapt to a certain level of tension on a regular basis. Then, when that stress intensifies, we can unconsciously adjust to the next level without even realizing it's happening.

And that kind of chronic stress can be treated in either healthy or unhealthy ways.

In America especially, many people overeat as a response to stress. Obesity has become a major epidemic affecting both children and adults, causing surges in related health problems like diabetes. Stress can also too easily lead to equally unhealthy and often connected sedentary lifestyle, where we're too exhausted at the end of the day to do anything other than collapse onto our couch and stare blankly at a screen.

It's easy for anyone to lose focus on a proper diet and exercise regimen. Again, think of busy parents with young children or those working co-vocationally. Both of these circumstances affect the family schedule and preparation of meals. People in the same household are going in multiple directions at any given time whether to work, school or other activities on the calendar. Many families no longer sit down to eat together at the evening dinner table. Menu planning is more about whether to stop at McDonald's or Wendy's than worrying about whether everyone is getting their daily quotas of fruits and vegetables.

Of course, some clergy do eat a proper diet and exercise regularly. However, there are other times when they neglect such regimens, often putting them on the back burner after everyone else's needs. Not to mention that almost every church dinner I've ever been to is a virtual banquet of carbohydrates and sweets, including leftovers that are packaged up to take home and finish later.

And, being a self-confessed chocolate lover, I often receive gifts of chocolate candy, which I totally appreciate. But I have to regulate my consumption, or I will eat the whole box too fast, binging on the sugar.

During my last pastorate, I even went so far as to hire a nutritionist to learn how to prepare and eat foods that serve my body better. Yet before long, I found that having to constantly monitor my diet and stick to an exercise routine was just another stressor on top of my already busy schedule. I quickly lost interest even though it would have been the best thing for me in the long run.

This is an issue I've since tackled, but at the time, especially when I ate meals alone, it was too quick and easy to run to a convenience store or fast-food restaurant to grab a bite – not the healthiest food by far. Too much of that on a regular basis also puts on weight from processed foods that are filled with sugar and sodium. These establishments are now required to give nutritional information about their products. It can be an eye-opening experience to stand in the line and read the calorie count or grams of sugar in what you are about to order.

Truth is, even though we know better, we don't always do better.

Added to all this is the tremendous strain on many pastoral families due to the lack of financial stability, including tension from living on less for long periods of time. Some ministry students leave university or seminary with school debt that's equal to a home mortgage. Yet if they pursue the calling to lead a church, their first assignment (and maybe many after) may not pay enough to adequately meet all their financial needs.

As a result, some choose not to pastor a church, opting instead for another way to express their call as an educator, counselor or the like.

Or they might become co-vocational, leading a church while also working at another part-time or full-time job to supplement their income. This is a big task.

Add to that the critical need to have insurance benefits. Many small churches can no longer afford to provide coverage to their pastor and his or her family. So, some must rely on insurance benefits offered either by a second job or a spouse's employer. Otherwise, they can't afford the cost of private health care for themselves or their family.

I must say that I am always so impressed by the commitment these co-vocational pastors have. So, let me take a moment here to challenge their congregations. These pastors need people in their churches who appreciate how hard the demand is to balance work, family and church. They need people who will help them in the process, doing the work of ministry they are gifted to do as staff or laity, and extending grace when not everything they expect of a pastor can be done.

I wish every layperson would come alongside their pastor this way. And the same is true for laity themselves, who often give many volunteer hours at their church after a long day at their job. It's a mutual sacrifice to build up the church in cooperative and collaborative labor.

This relationship between a pastor and the people is unique. Leading and managing a core of volunteers can be both exhilarating and challenging. But the truth is, most people I've worked with are kind-hearted and truly want to wholeheartedly follow God.

As for when they don't act like the followers of Christ they profess to be, I try to remember how Jesus dealt with his disciples, offering accountability with grace and compassion rather than condemnation or ridicule. This helps me avoid becoming a stress-mess myself. Plus, it aids me to think well of others – something that is worth a mention in and of itself.

I once sat at a table with ministers from a variety of denominational backgrounds. We were at a conference and during the break two men next to me began discussing people from their church. Apparently, a family had moved from one guy's church to the other guy's church.

And their comments about these folks were very unkind. Even though I understood that they were in a moment of "pastoral camaraderie", it made me wonder how they would be able to minister well to individuals who they had so obviously written off, even though they were difficult people to deal with.

Nor should we think that complaining about others is something only male pastors do. While I don't particularly like to mention it, I feel compelled to speak to some clergywomen I've met who constantly whine and moan about how awful it is for them and how excluded they feel.

I GET IT.

But I say to you ladies, you are only hurting yourself. If God has called you, stop whining and put into practice the skills, gifts and talents you have been graced with to serve the kingdom. Offer up to the Lord what you thought ministry would be like, allowing the creative possibilities of a mighty God to reveal to you what he thinks it can be like. You might be astounded! I know I was!

The creative imagination of God totally impacted how my years in ministry played out. For example, ever since I was a little girl, I insisted that I would never live in a big city. I didn't want to be in the crowds, the traffic, or the close housing quarters. And where did I end up? God lead me to serve in urban Philadelphia, Pennsylvania.

In the first church I pastored, there were 35,000 homes within a one-mile radius from the church and 3,700 students in the high school across the street, speaking over 37 different languages. Hardly the idyllic neighborhood I'd pictured.

But I ended up serving in various ministries in that city for 12 years, and I loved every minute of it! My life in Christ was shaped and strengthened there. He used my strengths and capabilities to glorify Him and engage the work of the kingdom. It was because of this experience that I learned a great lesson… Never say never.

God has an amazing sense of humor! He led me into places and situations I never imagined. And he will do the same for you.

Now, going back to the issue of whining, I do not wish to demean the need for systemic change that allows women to use their gifts. I'm fully aware that many qualified clergywomen never get opportunities to serve in accordance with their calling. I understand, and I feel for you.

I'm only suggesting that if you are reading this as a clergywoman, you may be pleasantly surprised at how your calling can evolve even when it's so unlike anything you expected. There are opportunities everywhere! But if we are stuck in negativity, those possibilities will be hidden to us or, at the least, no one will want to employ us. Not because we're female – because we're whiny and negative.

Which leads to the idea that for pastors in general, our perspective on God's calling is so very important. We have to decide at some point who we're serving.

I know… That sounds obvious. Of course, we're serving the Lord. But I can tell you how easily craving status or recognition within the systems we operate in can distract us. We want to be seen, to be heard, to be appreciated. And I have felt all of these things too at one time or another, some more than others.

However, in every situation, I've had to recognize and purposefully remind myself of this truth – I serve an audience of ONE. If I've done the best I know how and truly desire in my heart to glorify the Lord, then nothing else matters. I take my hurts and disappointments to him. He knows. He listens. And he wraps me with compassionate love.

This will not solve the systemic problem, but it surely meets the need for significance.

Not to mention how, trying to please people or get their attention takes up so much time and energy, and causes much more stress than focusing wholeheartedly on God. The Lord will give us the resources we need, including other pastors who can often much better understand what we're going through.

When we are together, there is a camaraderie among us that's unique because of the vocation we're in. Put simply, we need each other. And our conversations, even seemingly negative ones like that between the two men talking at the table, are understood in a way that those outside pastoral ministries can't comprehend. We don't expect them to understand.

And our personal relationships can be skewed by this reality.

Think about it... when a minister leaves a church assignment, his or her entire social network is also left behind. The people they have fellowshipped with - have lived life with - don't go with them. And if they don't have friends at church, then who are their friends outside that circle? Who do they go to when they're hurting or just need to process or talk through something that's happening?

In other words, *who is the pastor to the pastor?*

I once participated in a group dialog where the question was considered: Should a pastor have close friends who are church members? Can we have healthy relationships without blurring the lines or showing favoritism, or becoming too vulnerable to people who might turn on us or hurt us?

It was a lively discussion for sure! Some said we *must* have these relationships. Others declared, "No. No way. Never." Every pastor has to decide for himself or herself.

Along the same lines, maintaining a positive mindset about problematic people is a monumental task for anyone in any vocation. It's true that some people will suck the life out of you if you let them. But we can be encouraged not to completely give up on people – Jesus doesn't. This is a hazard of ministry to be avoided. We must keep on believing in others like Jesus believes in us or we risk becoming bitter and cynical, not giving others a chance to do and be what God has called them to do and to be.

Every year, as we celebrate Holy Week during the Easter season, I am intrigued by two images. One is the last supper scene, where Judas is given a seat at the table even though Jesus already knows he's the disciple who will betray him. This openness, this grace, this love is amazing to me. I'm not sure I would want to eat with Judas knowing what Jesus knew. He was, after all, the betrayer.

But there he is. And Jesus quietly allows him to reveal himself. No big drama. Just "go do what you have to do."

Amazing.

The second scene is that of the fickle crowd that follows Jesus as he comes into Jerusalem. Early in the week, they're waving palm branches and shouting "Hosanna! Blessed is he who comes in the name of the Lord!" (Mark 11:9). Within just a few days, they are shouting to Pilate, "Crucify him! Crucify him!" (Luke 23:21)

And Jesus' response to all this?

Father, forgive them...

WOW. Now that's a profound leadership lesson.

So, there it is again. We learn from the example of Christ how to treat people who don't treat us well. And when we find that being kind or extending forgiveness has become difficult – when we're avoiding people who are difficult or snapping at others – perhaps it's time to think about withdrawing to a solitary place for a vacation, or at least a nap!

March 3, 1979

Our Wedding Day

It gets better every day we're together.

CHAPTER 13

THE MAN WHO RIDES WITH ME

"So where is your church?"

My husband has been asked this so many times as people who meet us automatically assume that he's the pastor and I'm the spouse. This happened as recently as a few weeks before writing this when we visited a new church.

"My wife is the pastor," Ron will say, and points to me; a response that generates a variety of interesting reactions. Most are warm and welcoming, though some are downright comical. You can read the confusion on the person's face. Often there's a brief pause, followed by, "Really? How long have you been in ministry?" Believe it or not, a lot of people have never met a woman pastor before. So they're usually surprised when I tell them it's been 25 years.

Ron and I have had some great experiences in ministry over those years. They started in 1994 during my first pastoral assignment serving on staff in my home church. And they've provided some good laughs along the way, like the time we were invited to the annual Pastors and Wives Retreat.

As it so happened, Ron was the only male spouse of clergy there, since I was the only female minister present. It was really kind of cute how the days unfolded, repeatedly indicating how we were apparently the first role-reversed couple to ever attend. This meant it was a learning experience for everyone involved.

On the second day of our sessions, for instance, wives were directed to go to another room for their activities while the pastors met together. That led to the group-wide realization that Ron would be with the women and I would be with the men – an arrangement that no one was quite sure what to do with right away.

It was a little pothole in the road that shook people up for a moment. But they recovered quickly with no one worse off for the experience.

There was another such moment toward the end of the retreat when tokens of appreciation were being given out to everyone. The leader realized at the last minute that the homemade salad dressing kit was probably not the best gift for Ron.

What a hoot!

We had a good laugh and ultimately paved a new way for clergy to fellowship together. The very next year, the retreat was renamed, and it's been the Ministers and Mates Retreat ever since. I'm happy that our presence there was instrumental in redefining the culture we serve within. And it's so different now, with many more clergywomen and spouses around us.

Even so, there are other aspects that will probably never change, one of them being the scrutiny those ministerial mates live under just by virtue of being married to a pastor. That's particularly true for female spouses, since they often find themselves held up against a whole list of occupational and appearance-related expectations. There's even an old stereotype-turned-joke about these women that's often used in a lighthearted, loving way; jesting that a pastor's wife must be able to play the piano and wear a bun in her hair.

Unfortunately, there are many other less-lighthearted expectations out there as well. Many clergy wives live under the confines of people's beliefs about who they should be and what role they should play in the church, rather than who they are as God created them to be. Each of them is uniquely created with certain gifts and graces. It's a big enough problem that I've heard women testify about how they had to be released from these expectations, if only in their own spirit. One pastor's wife, a hairdresser by trade, even had a whole routine she did with a fake hairpiece to make her bun – and her point – about what a pastor's wife is "supposed" to look like.

While we may laugh at the typecasting in good fun, it's really not that funny for the spouses who have to live with such unrealistic expectations from the congregation.

Some of the old stereotypes that had to change first weren't even because more women began entering the ministry. Rather, they started to change when otherwise "traditional" wives began to work outside the home in order to bring in much-needed financial support for the family.

As mentioned in an earlier chapter, for many pastors, their first jobs are at small churches that often cannot pay a decent salary, much less offer healthcare coverage that meets the needs of a growing family. And when there's also educational debt from a university or seminary involved, a pastor's family's finances can get even tighter.

Thus, for many, a spouse's ability to bring in additional income can be a key factor in accepting a pastorate. In turn, that meant that many pastors' wives could no longer accompany them on visitation calls or host lovely dinner parties at the parsonage. They simply didn't have the time.

The stereotype that they did, or should, seems to have faded some as a result. But there are plenty more that live on, and quite strongly too, like the expectation that they should be in attendance at every service, lead women's ministries or have perfectly behaved children.

Yet in all my years in ministry, I've never encountered a prevailing church-role related stereotype for the male spouse of a female pastor. There's never a question about whether he can sing or what hairstyle he should wear. In fact, congregants are sometimes confused about what role a male spouse will play at all.

How is he expected to minister alongside his wife? Should he just work and be the main financial supporter so that the church can hire the clergywoman for less pay than they otherwise would? This line of thinking tends to dovetail with other ones regarding what some people think are "normal" roles between men and women in the marriage relationship, with the man being the main breadwinner.

Also, is the spouse viewed as less of a man because his wife is the leader of the church? I once heard a discussion on a radio program about the impression made when a woman is driving with her husband next to her. They suggested that it creates an image of him as a loser who probably lost his driver's license for some reason or is too weak to stand up to his wife and take the wheel.

What!?

Clearly then, it's not just congregants who get puzzled. There's a lot of curiosity among some of my colleagues as well, as shown by the time a male pastor asked me very casually, "So what is it like for you to be the spiritual head of your household?"

At first, I was stunned that he thought this. But then I collected myself and smiled.

"You misunderstand my relationship with my husband," I told him. "My husband and I don't see things the way you're describing them. We have a mutual understanding about spiritual leadership in our home and life. I just happen to be the one called to ministry, and I'm also more extroverted than he is. Thus, you see me up front, not him.

"He's an introvert and prefers to serve in the background. But without him, I would not be who I am today. He's a man of great faith, has a deep prayer life, and is my greatest prayer warrior and biggest cheerleader."

My colleague got it then, and there were no hard feelings over the question.

Yet it still stands out starkly as something to be considered and discussed. The assumption was that, because I'm up front more than Ron, I was more spiritual. But that's just not so. Perhaps some of my female colleagues would say the same about their spouses.

I've learned through this that, because a woman pastor with a male spouse is outside the norm, typecasting can happen quickly based on deeply held stereotypes about gender roles – many of which may be totally inaccurate.

The truth is that some clergy spouses prefer a role that allows them to operate behind the scenes at church simply because that's how they're wired. After all, unless they've been hired as a co-pastor on staff, there should be no expectation that they're automatically included as part of the pastoral package. That's true across the board for both male and female pastor's spouses.

During one interview, when we were asked by the church board what Ron's role would be, we had the opportunity to reinforce that he would find his place in ministry just like any other layperson. In other words, they were hiring me, not him. Some board members told me later on that this was helpful. They had never had a female pastor before, and so they needed a little additional guidance on what to expect.

So, regardless of gender, if your pastor is married and you respect them, I encourage you to make sure to esteem their spouse just as much for all the support they offer in so many different ways. Your encouragement goes a long way to make them feel needed and loved just for who they are as a member of the church body.

As I told my colleague that day, my husband is the introvert to my extrovert. That's his dominant personality temperament. He serves the church quietly in the background, which is his favorite place to be. Like so many other introverts, Ron is usually uncomfortable being upfront. Sometimes very much so.

I remember both of us being called to the church platform one Sunday when the entire church staff was presented with Christmas gifts. By the time we left the stage, he was sweating and visibly affected from standing in front of everyone. After that, I respectfully asked that he not be put in that kind of position again. In other words, to not spontaneously ask him to come up front. They meant well, of course, but the results didn't bless Ron quite the way they intended.

Because of a learning disability that affects his reading comprehension, he also doesn't like to be called on to read out loud, preferring to instead volunteer when he's so inclined. And, once again falling into the typical – yes, even stereotypical – introvert's profile, he favors one-on-one conversations rather than large group chats. It's just who he is, a consideration that should be factored in with any individual, pastor's spouse or not.

As the pastor, I've definitely tried to help people get to know Ron while still letting him be who he is. I've found it's helpful to reinforce his strengths and the ways he likes to serve through informal conversations, and then allow him to be himself and let people celebrate that with us.

Usually, other introverts in the church understand Ron well. But again because of some people's preconceived ideas about how men are supposed to function in relation to their wives, he has at times been placed in other situations that were very uncomfortable for him. This includes being asked academic-level theological questions as if he should know the answers to them.

Even so, one of the biggest things I've had to learn early on in ministry is not to answer for him. I can't tell you how many times I've since responded to people asking me whether he's available for such and such with, "I don't know. You'll have to ask him." I don't speak for him when someone asks if he can do something for the church or participate in a particular way. That's for him to decide.

Shouldn't it be for any spouse?

Ron and I have had many talks together over the years about boundaries, especially about how to properly deflect people who prefer to go to a man for answers rather than come to me as the leader of the church. He had to learn quickly how to interpret and refer questions to me that are pastoral in nature.

We've also had to talk through times when he directed someone about something, and I would have preferred he bring the situation to me. This was never done to purposely usurp me, but finding our individual and spousal strides in this regard did take some time. In conversations with others at church, Ron is careful to respect my leadership. He totally gets it, and I love him for it. But it isn't always easy for him, and it always required lots of communication between the two of us.

We also had to learn together how to create boundaries in our home, especially when his work required him to go to bed before dark and get up before daylight. And there were recurring conversations about what it's like for each of us to be a married couple while also pastor and congregant. We've never expected the rest of the congregation to completely understand the relational dynamics that ministry causes to our marriage. But we have found that, if we're clear with each other, it usually translates well enough to everyone else.

Now, this doesn't mean we never have conflicts that relate directly to church or ministry. There have been situations with people from church that affected us at home, and it's been difficult when we didn't agree about how to handle them. Similarly, there have been times of tension for me in being Ron's wife first and foremost, even though I'm also his pastor. That, in particular, is likely a strain at times for pastors of either gender.

Then there are the decisions that need to be negotiated between us about time, relationships, travel, and leadership styles, just to name a few. As with every other pastor/pastor's spouse couple – or husband and wife in general – we don't always see eye to eye. But we do remain committed to working it out the best we can when controversies arise.

Over the years, I have made it my goal to keep Ron from being assigned to a role or delegated a task at church just because he's the pastor's spouse. I also tried to guard against him having too much information, (e.g. sensitive issues discussed at a church board meeting), so that if he gets cornered by someone who assumes he knows the inside scoop on everything, he can honestly answer with, "I don't know." In this regard, I treat him like any other congregant.

None of this means I try to protect him because he's weak or vulnerable. Ron is a very self-confident man. He knows who he is, and he likes himself. There is no pretense with Ron. What you see is what you get, sometimes-goofiness and all. And if asked how he's doing, he is known for his standard answer of, "I'm doing superb, and I'm working my way up from there!"

I love his authenticity and positivity, and so do others. But that positivity doesn't mean he's always available for anyone's beck and call. Not even mine.

While I was doing pastoral ministry, Ron was employed as a dock builder for the carpenter's union. That meant he was working long hours in extreme temperatures doing heavy construction along with the 24-7 life of being my spouse. He would go to bed at 8:00 p.m. to be up at 3:00 a.m., so there were some church events that he simply could not attend.

He wanted to support me but couldn't always take off from work to do so for professional reasons, not to mention the loss of income it would mean. His was an hourly wage, not a salaried position; so every hour off cost us a lot in both income and benefits. Midweek retreats were almost impossible because of this.

So how did we handle it?

Ron suggested we develop a mutually beneficial guideline to help us navigate what I needed from him in ministry. We agreed that, if there was an event I had to attend like a staff dinner or annual district assembly meeting, it was my responsibility to tell him whether I really needed him to come along.

Denominational events are an especially good example of this because, years ago, it was an expectation that your spouse would attend with you. That has relaxed a lot over time since so many spouses work; but back when I first started out, that really wasn't considered much. So I would tell Ron either that I really needed him to come if he could; that, this time, it didn't matter at all; or I'd like him to come but it wasn't exceptionally important.

This set us both free from self-imposed constraints about what he should do to support me in ministry. And I chose not to get upset if he couldn't attend events even when I wished he could. After all, he had a hard job and needed rest and time off too. So we negotiated regularly on how to handle these situations the best way for our family.

Ron is also a gifted artist and skilled in fine carpentry, and his many talents are evident in the churches where I've served as pastor. He likes being given a task and then left alone to work it out. From putting new chandeliers up in the sanctuary to installing kitchens, taking on major projects to improve the parsonages we've lived in, and growing and sharing yummy vegetables in the summer, Ron's life has touched the people of every congregation we served.

He serves the Lord well with his gifts. Again, he's usually in the background with them, barely even noticed. But he's there nonetheless and making a difference in big and small and very appreciated ways.

In our last church, for instance, he could be found every Sunday standing in the doorway by the foyer in the back of the sanctuary while I preached. Ron kept a close eye on who came into the church and was alert to potential security issues as people passed by the ushers and greeters at the front door. This was a task he enjoyed. It was his way of watching out for me and the congregation in case something unexpected happened.

There are no words to express how grateful a clergyperson should be for a spouse who supports what God has called them to be and do. I have often said that I don't know how someone who is married could be a pastor without the support of his or her spouse. That support is expressed in many different ways depending on the person and situation. But it makes such a difference nonetheless.

Of course, I am very aware that some pastors don't have that luxury. There are some spouses, both male and female, who never adapt to life in the ministry. This can make a pastor's job doubly difficult. For example, many pastors assume that they and their families will likely move locations more than once during their ministerial career. Even so, this can get complicated when their spouse has a great job or there is a concern about moving children from school to school.

On the one hand, that husband or wife can choose to leave their employment to relocate with their pastor-mate. But not everyone will. And some won't, no matter what. The pastor then has few options outside of their current assignment, assuming that assignment even continues…

Naturally, that dilemma is much different from those faced by single clergy members, as several of my friends and acquaintances are or have been. Some have never been married at all. Others were, but lost their spouse either through death or divorce. No matter why they are single though, they tell me that there are distinct advantages and disadvantages to being unmarried in a pastoral role.

One advantage is being able to live and work independently, not worrying about when someone else needs dinner or expects them to be home. They only have to take care of themselves, including laundry, schedules, meals, and so on. The downside, of course, is the same: There is no one to come home to, which means there's no one to process thoughts or share stories with. Income is also more limited, as is emotional support and physical contact.

I need to state here that my single clergy friends are not unhappy. They just operate with different pros and cons than I do. And we all work with what we have or don't have.

Since I do have a marriage, and a strong one at that, it opens up a whole other set of responsibilities that Ron and I have discussed many, many times before. Over the years, we realized the opportunity we have to present to the church a model for a healthy marriage. After all, isn't that important for any leader to showcase, if they can?

This is not something we even remotely take for granted. Having both been divorced before, we know how much God has blessed our relationship.

When it comes to our "how we met" story – which, as you may remember, was at a bar years before we became Christians – we're once again not the typical pastoral couple. Yet Ron and I know for sure that it was the Lord who brought us together in that moment more than 46 years ago. And we know it is only by the divine providence of God that we've been able to develop such a strong second marriage since.

Over the years, we've met many couples who tell us they long for the kind of close relationship we have, making us that much more conscious of the example we get to set in that regard. In similar fashion, Ron has modeled for both men and women what it means to respect me as a woman and his wife in the pastoral role. And, in turn, I am always conscious of lifting him up as a man of God and showing him equal respect, letting him know how much I truly appreciate him.

I say these things to brag on God, not ourselves. This is all his doing.

But by far, the greatest gift Ron gives me is his willingness to listen. Obviously, there are some matters that come to me as a pastor that I simply cannot discuss with him. But when it comes to processing my thoughts in general, I am an out-loud thinker, which he very well knows. So many times, after I return from a conference or trip, he greets me with, "Tell me all about it." Then he sits and listens to me babble about people he'll never meet and all the things that happened that would otherwise be of no interest to him outside of supporting me.

I often thank him for just listening when I'm processing a sermon or making plans for something new as well. Actually, I used to think I talked too much, but he reassured me that, when I don't communicate with him, he feels left out. He says that these talks help him know where I am and what I'm thinking.

Naturally, the same is true when I listen to him talk about things that are important to him, like gem mining or creating a new gadget he can use to make a particular job easier. It's a mutual thing with us. But I often tell him I'd go crazy with my own thoughts without his listening ear.

Plus, since I purposefully select sermon illustrations with consideration to the average male congregant as well as the average woman, Ron has helped me develop ideas that relate to topics he knows more about than I do, like carpentry or tools.

I also trust his standard male perspective on people. For example, he sees more quickly than I do if someone is taking advantage of me. I have asked him before about certain men who want to hug me at church – what do you sense from them? (And he will ask me about the women who want hugs from him.)

And, very importantly, I've learned to listen when he tells me I'm overworking myself. Ron knows me better than anyone else in my life, and I tend to be driven and go at things until I drop. So, I know that by the time he says something, I'm well over the edge and he's now truly concerned about me. I used to resist hearing this feedback from him, but now I recognize his voice as one of love and care, and I listen and respond accordingly. It's a good feeling to know he's in my corner watching out for me on every level, including physically and emotionally. There are times I just don't see how hard I'm pushing myself.

I know I've said this before, but it bears repeating – Ron is also my strongest prayer partner. He usually has more faith than I do. His temperament is cool when mine runs hot. And he's calm when I'm obsessing. I cannot imagine this life without him, and I cannot thank God enough for the support he has given me all these years.

Ron is my best friend on earth, and I know he loves me unconditionally.

We refer to ourselves as "a couple of individuals" – two people who are very different from one another but celebrating those differences together every day of the rest of our lives. And when we travel in the car, sometimes he drives and sometimes I drive, and neither of us cares, as long as we get where we're going safely.

The way we see it, we can't be lost on the ride as long as we're together.

Clothes aren't going to change the world.

The women who wear them will.

- Anne Klein

CHAPTER 14

TRAVEL CLOTHES

Never go to the store with curlers in your hair.

That's just one of the lessons my mother taught me about how to present myself in public that I've lived by all my life.

For some women, it's to never leave the house without your makeup properly applied. Or maybe you grew up with the old adage: Always have on clean underwear in case you're in an accident.

Yes, those proverbial lectures on the public presentation of self.

Now if you came to my house and looked in my dresser drawer, you'd find an old, silver-colored sweater. It was a hand-me-down from my daughter when she was in high school. She graduated in 1990, which gives you some idea of how old this sweater is.

Purchased from a store that has long since gone out of business, the hems of the sleeves and bottom are tattered, with threads hanging loose like tinsel on a Christmas tree. It's no longer fit for public viewing, and I wear it only in the house on days when I'm cleaning or just hanging out. Yet while I have about 10 other sweaters that are newer, warmer and without a single loose thread, I prefer this silver mess over all of them.

It is by far the most comfortable one I own.

Even so, I would never consider wearing it in public. Mother simply would not have approved. She taught me that there are certain acceptable ways to dress depending on where you are going and what the occasion is.

You see, because my father was a disabled veteran, we lived on a very fixed income with Mom being the master of the monthly budget.

We simply did not spend money lavishly. It was only every now and then that Mom and Dad would take my two brothers and me shopping. After all, we were growing and needed new clothes as a result.

There was one particular store in our town called The New York Apparel Shop. It was run by a Jewish family who, I'm sure now, actually *went* to New York to buy the clothes. I didn't even know where New York was back then, so it certainly never occurred to me that the inventory came from someplace so exciting. All I knew was that it was a girls' store. Mom would trudge in with me at her side to tell them what she wanted, whereupon the wife would lead us to the right-size racks.

At Easter, however, The New York Apparel Shop was left behind for an afternoon adventure at Robert Hall Clothiers. The whole family would pile into the station wagon and go on an excursion to purchase suits for the boys and a fancy dress for me. These were our Easter outfits for church.

Of course, they had to be practical enough to be worn again after the holiday. Mom and Dad couldn't afford to waste money on a one-time clothing gig. But we didn't care. It was a big day at our house.

My favorite part of that adventure was always shoe shopping. For that matter, I'm still a sucker for a good shoe sale. As an adult, I've had to develop a rule to keep my shoe inventory under control. If I buy a pair, I must designate them as replacement shoes and thus purge a pair from the closet when I get home. This helps controls my urges for that new, potential "must have" pair.

But I digress.

In the back of the Chevy again, after we'd made our purchases at Robert Hall Clothiers, a thirty-something minute ride would take us to the main drag of a low-budget town where the Kinney Shoe store beckoned us to "Come in! Come in. There's plenty of parking. Come in!"

Inside, rows and rows of shoes were just waiting to be tried on.

It was the bonanza of shopping because, if I was lucky (and I usually was), I got three pairs of shoes all in the same day! One was reserved for play, one for school and the third for church.

Every one of us kids understood the shoe system. Really, the separation of shoes for specific purposes was pretty normal for the day on top of being very practical for our family.

My play shoes were Keds sneakers. Always. They could be any color; though, of course, in the 1950s, there were only two or three to choose from – black, white or tan, I think – all with laces. No slip-ons. No fuchsia, tangerine or plaid. Just the basics.

The trick with Keds was to not get them wet, or at least not soaking wet. That made the rubber come off the sides too soon. And cleaning them was a planned affair because they took a long time to dry inside. That's right, we didn't have an automatic clothes dryer then either.

Clipped by their tongues on the backyard clothesline, good weather was a must for such a serious task. Winter was tricky because your shoes hung in the basement and took f-o-r-e-v-e-r to dry. And since we were never allowed to wear our school shoes or church shoes to play in, if our Keds weren't dry, then the last old, funky pair we used to wear was resurrected from the back of the closet.

Assuming we still had an old pair that fit.

Play shoes were meant for wear and tear. Getting filled with dirt in the sandbox. Heels drug on the ground under the swing or on the concrete sidewalk under bicycle pedals to come to a stop. Metal clips clamped to their sides for roller skating. Sliding into home plate in the back yard. Kicking footballs. Running in a game of tag. Under rubber boots in the winter (cold, cold, cold). Mud puddles on a rainy day – though not too many, considering how we'd then have to clean them and then wait f-o-r-e-v-e-r for them to dry.

Play shoes took a beating. But you didn't get yelled at for this, because that's what play shoes were designed for. They saved your other shoes for better things.

Now, my school shoes were what they called saddle shoes. Black and white and clunky by today's standards, they had thick, brown leather soles and laces up the front. I can't tell you what my brothers wore. I only know I wore saddle shoes. My mom said they were "sturdy"… just what every girl longs to be seen in.

At school, we were careful at lunchtime recess. Dodge ball, swings, tag, and ball games were played on the tar-covered playground with care not to scuff our footwear. Sometimes we were successful. Sometimes we weren't, in which case, we were responsible for cleaning them. That's why, in third grade, the craft to master was applying white and black liquid shoe polish without running them together.

Back then, I knew the rule that one just did not go to school with dirty shoes! It would make the family look bad. I mean, what kind of parents let their kids go to school in dirty shoes anyway?

(Though funny enough, I couldn't tell you today if anyone else had dirty shoes or not. Maybe my mother could have…?)

Lastly, I had a very special pair of shoes for church: patent leather Mary Janes that were very shiny. Black in winter; white in summer. These were the holy grail of my shoe collection.

Of course, girls didn't wear pants to church back then (or school, for that matter), so a pretty dress always topped off my Mary Janes. The minute I got home from church though, the dress came off to be hung in the closet and the shoes were neatly positioned back on the floor, not to be touched again until the next Sunday.

Really, I never remember wearing those shoes anywhere but church since special events were all inevitably held there anyway. School events weren't special enough. Seems like a waste now, since I always grew out of them so quickly.

But that's the story of how I was taught to wear acceptable occasion-specific outfits. Of course, the definition of "acceptable" has changed over the years.

When I was in business in the 1980s, women conformed to the corporate culture, wearing suits with blouses that tied in a bow at the neck. And very few wore flats; heels were in order. I remember the first time I read that the dress code for a work event was "business casual."

"What in the world is that?" I thought. Then it became "dressy casual". More new language to describe what was acceptable to wear. Then there was a "dress-down day" at work, perhaps on Fridays, when you could actually wear jeans if you wanted. Today, anything seems to go and the rules I learned so clearly aren't just fuzzy. They've been entirely erased.

I can't even remember the last time I saw a woman sporting curlers other than at a hair salon. We use curling irons now.

Likewise, lots of fashion changes have taken place over the span of my ministry. So when it comes to how to "appropriately" dress in church, I do understand that there can be expectations influenced by a person's age and upbringing. If a church is filled with people in their 60s or older, for example, they likely have pretty strong thoughts on what the pastor and other people on the platform should wear – even if they opt for a more casual look themselves. Meanwhile, for the 20 and 30-somethings, what church leadership wears doesn't seem to matter as much as what we have to say.

So how do we reconcile all this? What does it all mean in ministry today?

My personal opinions on this issue have been both strengthened and challenged by the entire conversation surrounding clothing and appearance in church. As times change, and fashions with them, I've grappled to find an acceptable "middle ground" both with congregants and colleagues alike.

So I offer these ideas as things to think about, not as rules for everyone. While I prefer to dress in what might be viewed as a more conservative style, each of us must find our own way in a culture that celebrates skintight leggings, miniskirts and low-rider jeans.

Let me begin though by talking a little bit about pastors in particular.

In the United States, a male pastor can show up to conduct a wedding ceremony or funeral service in a black suit and fit right in without wearing a clergy robe. Whereas a woman in a black suit can be criticized as looking too manly or severe. Yet to wear colorful clothes can be taken as too flashy or self-aggrandizing.

Especially at a wedding, a colorful dress can clash with the color of the bridesmaids' gowns. I mean, what if the presiding pastor wears a bright green outfit and the bridesmaids' gowns are fuchsia? And heaven forbid you wear white – that's for the bride! Whatever your ultimate choice, you don't want to stand out too much or be the center of attention. So what works?

I serve in a denomination where most clergy don't wear robes as their weekly pulpit garb. But I quickly learned that robes are a safer alternative for certain special occasions, weddings being high on the list. My first clergy robe was white with gold trim, and people loved to see me wear it. But I have to say, I didn't enjoy it. In fact, I felt lost in it.

It fit like a man's robe, with sleeves that were too baggy and long, and a body that was too full and wide for a smaller woman like me. And it was way too expensive to just go buy another one.

The same problems apply to clergy shirts with collars. When I served in an urban church, I often wore a collar to visit people in the metropolitan hospitals. This created instant credibility when introducing myself as a pastor. Yet the first shirt I bought had to be tailored so it didn't fit like a balloon top.

Fortunately, a friend of mine who's a seamstress put darts in the front for a more fitted look so I wouldn't feel sloppily dressed.

In recent years, it's been so great to see companies like WomenSpirit begin to make clergy robes, blouses and dresses to fit the shape of a woman's body much better. But that is now; this was then.

In presentation skills training classes during my business days, I'd always been coached to wear colors as a speaker to create an overall more pleasing presentation. Yet there is a fine line between wanting to be seen and *how* I want to be seen. As a preacher, I want to look nice, yes, but I don't want to be the center of attention. I want God's word and Jesus to be the focal point. So if congregants are distracted by what I'm wearing, it can interfere with them listening and really hearing what God wants to say.

Plus, in the pulpit, there are several considerations for women preachers that aren't commonly known. Jewelry, for example.

I can't tell you how many times I take off my necklace when I preach because the lapel microphone is clacking on the chain. When my sermons were being recorded, the noise was even distinctive enough to detract from the quality of the recording. The sound team would signal me if they heard the noise before I did, and we did have some good laughs over it. But I still thought about this potential problem every Sunday morning when getting dressed before church.

Incidentally, dangling or flashy earrings can also distract, especially if they reflect little beams of light onto the walls.

Then there's the question of where to attach the microphone pack when using a lapel mic. For the record, a dress with no waistband or belt leaves no place for the clip.

I made this mistake several times, including at a seminar where I was one of the guest speakers for an audience of about 400 people. Just before I was to go on stage, the sound person handed me the mic… which is when I realized I had not thought it out well enough.

I was wearing a dress with no obvious place to attach everything.

Due to slip-ups like that, I've wired microphones inside and out of my clothing many times just to keep them in place. I once even preached wearing the mic pack clipped to my dress at the top of my neck in the back. That was a big distraction for me, as I felt it moving around during the entire sermon to the point where I worried it would fall off.

That's just one part of the microphone dilemma. There's also the mic itself to consider. Put simply, if my dress or blouse doesn't have a front placket, there's no place to clip the mic without bunching up some fabric on the front. As such, I've ruined more than one blouse with mics that left black marks or tore the fabric. Over-the-ear mics resolve this problem, naturally. But even then, you still need a place to clip the mic pack.

Also problematic in this regard is how women's blouses button in the opposite direction of a man's shirt. This means that, when I'm preaching at a church that usually has a man in the pulpit and they hand me a lapel mic, I know that the position of the clip will be backwards and need to be reversed before I put it on. Otherwise, it will be upside down.

The sound technicians can get pretty confused by this unexpected switch. I've been looked at like I'm crazy a time or two, to say the least.

As a guest preacher, I was even once handed a mic pack that had no clip on it at all. The regular pastor always put it in his pants or jacket pocket when he preached. So since I wasn't wearing an outfit with pockets that morning, I ended up using the hand-held microphone instead.

Above and beyond all of those hassles, I personally believe that, for all women, our outfits should be fashionable and up-to-date, yet counter-cultural in modesty. Yet I personally see how this is getting harder all the time. I think this is one of the smart things about the Salvation Army: They know what uniform to wear, and that's it.

Not so with most other professions and occasions. Try finding a beautiful conservative dress to wear to a wedding reception, for instance. Most fancy dresses are sleeveless these days, and I entered the ministry in an era where I was told bare arms are a distraction.

That's right. I was once questioned by another pastor, a man, about why I came to work wearing a sleeveless blouse on a hot and humid summer day. He said that showing that much skin was considered inappropriate for a pastor. This was news to me – didn't he know it was hot outside?

More culture shock. That a sleeveless blouse would be considered inappropriate never entered my mind, and his remarks conditioned me to feel uneasy about it ever since.

So you can see how far some take this.

Although it's advisable to have some sort of boundaries, we still grapple with where that line should be.

For example, today, many women's dresses and tops feature plunging V-necks purposefully designed to show off cleavage. And if you listen to fashion commentators on TV, you will often hear the word "sexy" used to describe a favorable look. But as Christian women, we're to be aware of how much is too much to show. Exposing a lot of cleavage can invite the wrong kind of attention, even from well-meaning males.

And if we don't have 20-year-old legs anymore, we probably shouldn't go around in dresses and skirts that don't fit our age. Frankly, I think some dresses and skirts are even too short when you do have 20-year-old legs!

My point is that there's a difference between dressing to look seductive versus wearing feminine and attractive apparel.

I know some will call me an old fuddy-duddy for my opinion. And I will once again acknowledge how difficult finding even reasonably modest clothing can be. Women's clothing fabrics these days are commonly see-through, designed with that "sexiness" in mind instead of enhancing our natural beauty. So finding something modest may come down to a dress that is so plain it can feel more like you're wearing a sack than something up-to-date and attractive.

This leads me to another annoying caveat I need to mention, since, believe it or not, even just looking too feminine can backfire. Like the mic situation, I know this from personal experience.

I once attended a big meeting in which I had a key leadership role. I usually dress in slacks for work meetings, but it was a beautiful day in early spring, so I decided to wear a light blue top with a skirt of the same color, printed with a floral design.

I realized afterward that, with some in the group, this choice of clothing affected my image as a strong leader. Except for me, the group was comprised of all men. One man even casually joked about my "girly" outfit. Looking at it now, I realize I would have done better to stick with a plain suit or slacks and a jacket. It would have strengthened my image as a leader in that particular meeting.

Sounds silly, I know. But as exasperating as it was, it did happen - and still does – further complicating the question of what's appropriate to wear when.

And what about makeup? How much is enough, and how much is too much?

Some women won't be seen in public without makeup on. Others prefer to wear none at all, and that's beautiful. For me though, I feel as if I look tired and much older without it.

My husband jokes with me that I don't need to put it on, and I joke back that I was wearing makeup when he met me and I probably always will. But he still won't kiss me if I'm wearing lipstick! So that's a different kind of tradeoff for adding color to my face.

That aside, the real question is whether our makeup adds to our beauty or detracts from it. For example, some women can bravely and beautifully wear black lipstick. But I'm not sure that's the best choice for a place like the pulpit if you want people to listen to your words and not be thinking about your lip color.

The impact of such choices may vary based on your audience. After all, a group of teens will probably think nothing of what others would consider to be outrageous makeup. But a congregation filled with lots of senior adults may take issue with it and stop listening altogether.

Again, we each have to find our way in this: to be ourselves and not conform to what other people think we should do or be. At the same time, it's important to consider what impact our makeup or lack thereof can have on being heard and seen as credible.

Another newer cultural expression like this is multi-colored hair. Some find it hideous; some think it's cool. All of which, believe it or not, brings us right back around to the too-much-skin-showing thing.

I realize that fashion has changed. I said so before, and I'll say it again. It always does, and it always will. But as women, should we really put men, who we know are more visual creatures than us, in the position where they have to constantly be wishing we'd cover up? Or worse yet, telling us to cover up?

That is a more-than-awkward conversation to have. For anyone.

Some women reading those last few lines may now be shouting at me for saying such things – another indication of how emotion-charged this whole discussion can be. So let me clarify.

Ladies, I'm not suggesting that we are responsible for how a man reacts to us, no matter what we wear. In our culture, women have been ingrained with the idea that we are responsible for enticing a man. It's been communicated, both subtly and overtly, that it's our job to protect men from fantasizing about us and sinning as a result.

That's ridiculous.

Men are responsible for themselves. And we are responsible for ourselves.

Rather, my intent is to look at these issues in the spirit of I Corinthians 10:23, where the Apostle Paul says:

> "I have the right to do anything," you say – but not everything is beneficial. "I have the right to do anything" – but not everything is constructive.

Paul reminds us that we all have free will to make choices. It seems, though, that we should consider whether our choices help or hinder. Is choosing to dress in a certain way beneficial or constructive? This goes for ourselves and others.

As for me, I've had to have conversations with women who sit facing forward on the platform during worship service, asking them to make sure they keep their knees together when they sit up front. There have been other times when I wanted to tell women to cover their cleavage in church. For me, this is no different than asking people to keep from talking inside the sanctuary during service – or any number of other things that can detract people's attention from worshipping the Lord.

Yet how do you approach doling out such advice? The conversation can be painfully difficult, even among family members, much less from a non-related man to a woman or a pastor to a congregant. No matter how well-intentioned the advice-giver is, the recipient might associate it with a selfishly motivated opinion that only makes them feel worse.

Debra Tannen, author and linguist, gives such an example as she recites one such mother-daughter conversation in her book *You're Wearing That?*[1]

> Loraine was spending a week visiting her mother, who lived in a senior living complex. One evening they were about to go down to dinner in the dining room. As Loraine headed for the door, her mother hesitated.
>
> Scanning her daughter from head to toe, she asked, "You're not going to wear that, are you?"
>
> "Why not?" Loraine asked, her blood pressure rising. "What's wrong with it?"
>
> "Well, people tend to dress nicely for dinner here, that's all," her mother explained, further offending her daughter by implying that she was not dressed nicely.
>
> Her mother's negative questions always rubbed Loraine the wrong way because they so obviously weren't questions at all. "Why do you always disapprove of my clothes?" she asked.
>
> Now her mother got that hurt look, which implied it was Loraine who was being a cad. "I don't disapprove," she protested, "I just thought you might want to wear something else."

How many of us can relate to such barbed comments to some degree or another?

Even my truly sweet mother offered her own version of, "You're not wearing that, are you?" on the night of my ordination as an elder in the church. I had a new dress ready to put on, but at the last minute, discovered there was a button missing on the front. With a limited wardrobe in my hotel room, I had little else to choose from. So I opted to put on a skirt suit – which was not what I'd planned to wear.

Already feeling self-conscious that the length of the skirt might be too short when I sat down, my mother added to my angst by saying, "I don't like that suit, Shirley. You don't look like *my* daughter."

I've never forgotten those words. They put a damper on the entire evening. It felt awful to think that someone whose approval was so important to me was disapprovingly focused on how I looked, particularly on such a momentous occasion.

The point is that talking about how we dress can be potentially hurtful, even with people we love very much.

I know I once handled things poorly myself when, without much forethought, I asked one of the teens in our church to put on a sweater for the worship service to cover up her very revealing little crop top. In so doing, I hurt her deeply and caused a rift in our relationship that never went away.

Subsequently, I sent a letter to all the women of our congregation, addressing my concerns about how we dressed.

Being that our church was close to a university campus, I also had to make decisions as the pastor about college students who came to church barely covered up – knowing they saw nothing wrong with how they were dressed. Like me with my sleeveless blouse episode, it never occurred to them that showing so much skin could be a distraction to some people. Plus, these were new believers we were trying to minister to.

So what do you do? Where do you draw the line as the pastor when you can help or hurt a person by saying something, or hurt and offend others in the congregation by not saying anything? And if this is that hard for me to figure out, imagine being a man and having to address this with women in the congregation.

As mentioned before, even pastors' pulpit-attire has changed. Some pastors have stopped wearing suits altogether while preaching, and being in the pulpit with jeans is in vogue. So what do we tell young pastors who come to serve with us? What are the expectations of the congregation, which can vary from church to church or even by the region of the country you serve?

Do they matter?

Should we just let everyone wear what makes him or her comfortable, and leave it at that?

I think we do have a responsibility to show what a professional person looks like as the leader of the church. But how does a "professional person" dress today? Everything is so much more casual than before.

Each person has to answer those questions for themselves, but I think we should give thought to what kind of example we set. In a thoughtful, Godly way, we can consider others as we decide how to present ourselves. I remember when a married male member of my church who was from another country told me that, in his culture, having the pastor dress well was an expectation.

To him, true leaders presented their best-dressed selves to God and the congregation. It was part of their job description.

It's an interesting thought, isn't it? Obviously, it can be taken too far, but I believe there's still a lot of truth to be found there.

Delving even further into different ways of thinking, I also learned along the pastoral way that not everyone believes women should wear pants. In my first church assignment, while serving a multi-cultural congregation, I preached in a dress or skirt for the entire five years out of respect for those who would be offended by anything less.

This choice was driven by the particular congregation I was serving, most of who came from another country and thus had different cultural ideas about how to dress in public. While some might think my decision was a bit overboard, I chose to do this because I wanted everyone to be comfortable inviting family and friends to the service and to be proud of, not embarrassed by, their pastor. I saw it as an expression of love and respect.

In other assignments, however, I rarely wore a dress to preach, as I am typically more comfortable in pants. And honestly, I've never quite figured out how to address the decline in wearing pantyhose, which provides at least a minimal covering for the legs. Somehow, having bare legs always feels strange to me.

But some of that's my age, no doubt, as well as another left-over from both my business career and ministerial paradigms. Most women regularly now dress up for even the fanciest occasions with bare legs. So again, I think it's a matter of personal preference.

Another change I've seen in our particular denomination is that both laywomen and clergywomen of all ages wear shorts to church functions or even ministry conventions. Other pastors I know wear sloppy-fitting clothes or even dirty jeans to meetings.

Out in public, sweatpants have become acceptable garb, I know. And having lived in a university town for many years, I'm also well aware that pajama pants aren't uncommon in campus wardrobes. So clearly, the question of what role our personal presentations make applies outside of church just as much as inside.

Scripture says, "Your beauty should not come from outward adornment, such as elaborate hairstyles and the wearing of gold jewelry or fine clothes. Rather, it should be that of your inner self, the unfading beauty of a gentle and quiet spirit, which is of great worth in God's sight" (1 Peter 3:3-4, NIV). In The Passion Translation, it says, "Let your true beauty come from your inner personality, not a focus on the external" (1 Peter 3:3).

So there is clearly a balance needed between the beautiful person we are on the inside and the outward looks we try to enhance using makeup, clothing, or hairstyles. How we present ourselves is a sign of self-respect – or lack thereof. It should not be a decision based on an effort to please people or make an impression on others, even when it's seen as a sign of respect.

It's the Lord we should seek to please as we approach this delicate topic. How we dress is an act of worship that can glorify God and strengthen our witness, or it can detract from it. In the end, the reality is that it's so much more important to focus on what we're depicting through our personality and spirit than any outward expressions we use to make ourselves look presentable.

So here are my final thoughts on the subject...

I don't think we should become obsessed with this topic.

Pondering ourselves in the mirror too much can lead us to become self-conscious beyond reason. But unless we're holed up at home in our threadbare silver sweaters, our way of dress can and will affect others. Which does seem to indicate we should give some thought to the matter.

Especially if someone's receptivity to the gospel is on the line.

> If you want to lead the orchestra,
> you must be willing to turn your
> back to the crowd.
>
> *- Author Unknown*

EPILOGUE

I suppose every leader faces moments of insecurity, especially females who are sometimes told we don't have the right to do what we're doing.

As leaders of God's people, we can somewhat relate to Moses. Like those he led, sometimes our congregations or others around us will not want to hear what God has to say through us. But we have to say it anyway. We're called to.

Moses didn't have any of the self-awareness tools I discussed in previous chapters. He wasn't sure he saw himself doing all the things God saw him doing. As recorded in Exodus 3:11 and 4:1 respectively, Moses tried to convince the Lord not to call him, using questions like, "Who am I, that I should go to Pharaoh and bring the Israelites out of Egypt?" and "What if they do not believe me or listen to me?"

As paraphrased from Exodus 4:13, he even flat-out begged, "Oh Lord, please send someone else to do it."

Yet God's vision is always bigger than ours. He sees in us what we cannot see in ourselves. He leads us where we need to go for our good and his glory.

So where do we go to discover this revelation of God's vision? What do we do to comprehend how much leadership potential he has placed in us? To see ourselves as He sees us?

For any Christian, male or female, minister or not, it should go without saying that a personal devotional life is foundational to self-discovery and the revelation of God's will. Sometimes it comes easy. Sometimes it eludes us. However, when it comes, the response may be manifested in various ways, just like the people we read about in the Bible.

We find in the pages of Scripture those who, like Moses, cried out to God on a regular basis due to the difficulties surrounding them. We also encounter those, like David, whose spirits were lifted through pure worship, praise and singing to the Lord, even if they were all alone. We meet the obedient and the disobedient, the blessed and the cursed. A myriad of responses and results are portrayed depending on what someone sees, hears and follows – or not.

As for the habits of spiritual discipline, they work differently for everyone. Some like to journal, others pray for extended periods of time, and some sing or meditate quietly. Likewise, some like to encounter the Lord first thing in the morning, and some throughout the day, while still others prefer a quiet time in the evening.

No matter what the exact expression, the vitality of our devotional life is essential to sustain spiritual, emotional and psychological health. It serves as a key component of well-being and wholeness. Each person can experiment with and settle on the practice of spiritual disciplines that will help him or her encounter God and have truth revealed.

After all, nothing will shape us for the better like time in God's word and prayer. And nothing will drastically affect us for the worse like losing that connection. It's through Bible reading, prayer, and the intervention of the Holy Spirit that God offers us the stamina, wisdom and self-awareness needed to stay the course on this journey of life.

The nourishment we receive from being devoted to these disciplines strengthens us to live each day with "confidence in what we hope for and assurance about what we do not see" (Hebrews 11:1) Such faith very often involves just waiting on God to reveal what's next. Even though every Christian is subjected to this challenging dynamic at some point, the pastor – as the leader being counted on as the spokesperson for God to his or her people – especially needs to be in touch with the One holding the directions.

Times of waiting for God's direction can be stressful when we're anxious to map out a course of action but don't yet have the destination. Impatience can fester while we wait for more clear instructions. We may have to fight the urge to step on the gas pedal too soon. It's easy in these times to take matters in our own hands, drive off the highway and find ourselves in a spiritual ditch while trying to lead on God's behalf. We're better off to just be still, persevere in prayer, wait and listen.

And if, during a season like that, we can succumb to being driven by what others think of us. "What are we waiting for?" they might ask. And the answer may be, "I m not sure." If people don't understand the waiting, pressure can be applied to move before it's God's time to do so.

People-pleasing motivations can drive us right into an unhealthy trap of stepping out on our own strength and not God's, possibly overextending ourselves and/or the people of the church we're supposed to be serving. Living in such a state of anxiety all the time, worrying about what people think or what they're saying when we're not around, isn't beneficial to anyone. So rather than take action before God speaks simply because others are pressuring us, well, I'll say it again...

We're better off to just be still, persevere in prayer, wait and listen.

And then there's the "call to ministry" I've referred to throughout this book. My colleagues counseled me when I began this journey that it would be God's call on my life that would sustain me over the years. They were right. Pastoral work is not for the faint of heart.

It's the people part that makes it so complicated; yet that's the core of our labor. Everything we do is for the Lord and is about his people. This is a source of great joy in the ministry. We have the privilege of engaging with people in the midst of their most wonderful, and difficult, personal moments.

Along the way, we may find ourselves needing to work with people who are difficult or who don't understand us. And we'll likely deal with disagreements on a fairly regular basis. Yet conflicts are a normal part of life in general. They're inevitable whenever people are involved.

So clashes will happen. Expect them.

Believe it or not, we need those clashes. They can be good because they stretch us as we work to reach consensus or compromise. Yes, it can be hard to think beyond the frustrations of the immediate situation. And yes, we need to find ways to develop our conflict resolution skills. But leaders who can model healthy ways to resolve conflicts in light of biblical truths can really teach people a different way than they're used to.

We teach them Jesus' way.

Whenever disputes arise, just think of how many disagreements Moses faced over his leadership! Just one of many examples is recorded in Exodus 16:2…

> In the desert the whole community grumbled against Moses and Aaron. "If only we had died by the Lord's hand in Egypt! There we sat around pots of meat and ate all the food we wanted, but you have brought us out into this desert to starve this entire assembly to death."

And again, when the people wanted water, they grumbled so badly that Moses cried out to the Lord: "What am I to do with these people? They are almost ready to stone me." (Exodus 17:4)

Literally at his wit's end with these fickle Israelites who were, don't forget, the people God called him to lead, notice how Moses constantly confessed his troubles and weaknesses to the Lord. He kept getting in God's face. He stayed focused on what God could do – he knew who his power really came from.

This brings us right back to how imperative it is to stay focused on God. Not ourselves. Not other's approval. Just God. Because when pastors lose that connection, they can become self-righteous and unhealthy and cause irreparable damage to God's people.

In her book, *Rising Strong*[1], Brené Brown raised a question that stopped me in my tracks when I read it:

"Do you think, in general, that people are doing the best they can?"

Facing that question has helped me dig deep inside myself for compassion at times when I didn't think I had any left. And sometimes, I need to apply that compassion to myself as well. Because I too am really just doing the best I can. What else is there?

Let's face it. People will not always agree with our leadership. At some point or another, they're likely to have their own versions of "take us back to Egypt – it was better there" – or the opposite of, "take us to the Promised Land already. Let's get going!" But no matter which rendition of the journey they're expressing at the moment, both sets are looking to us for leadership regardless.

Admittedly, there are times of prolonged difficulty when pastors would rather quit. And many do. Some go on to find other ways to express their call outside of being a church pastor. Others give up on it altogether, as widely circulated statistics indicate.

But there are many others who *don't* quit. They don't feel led to. And so they stick it out for the long term. There are many who have been at it for 20, 30 or even over 50 years. Pastors who are just starting out or who need extra encouragement or insight along the way can learn a lot from them.

They'll remind us that, when we are discouraged, the voice of God in our ear can keep us going if only we will listen and follow. And they'll also provide examples of how our calls do not make us superhuman or even super-spiritual. When we suffer, we do not have to be silent martyrs, steeping in our own misery. We're allowed to admit our failings and beg God for reassurance that he hasn't forgotten us.

Moses certainly went there. When he didn't feel like he could do all God asked of him, he said:

> "You have been telling me, 'Take these people up to
> the Promised Land.' But you haven't told me whom

you will send with me. You have told me, 'I know you by name, and I look favorably on you.' If it is true that you look favorably on me, let me know your ways so I may understand you more fully and continue to enjoy your favor. And remember that this nation is your very own people."[2]

And the Lord responded with this beautiful promise: "... 'I will personally go with you, Moses, and I will give you rest – everything will be fine for you.'"[3]

Now, that message didn't precisely translate how Moses must have envisioned it. At the end of his ministry, he didn't even get to enter the promised land! Yet everything was fine for him nonetheless. The fulfillment of his call came to rest on the fact that he followed God the best he understood based on his honest desire to enact the will of the Almighty.

That was enough. And it's enough for us too.

This is what our Savior desires. It's clearly stated in Deuteronomy 10:12-13...

> So now, O Israel, what does the Lord your God require of you? Only to fear the Lord your God, to walk in all his ways, to love him, to serve the Lord your God with all your heart and with all your soul, and to keep the commandments of the Lord your God and his decrees that I am commanding you today for your own well-being.

This is the path to living out our faith – the path to leadership wholeness.

The pastor's call is to follow God; to be who he wants us to be, and to let him shape us and use us for his glory. Then, no matter how we end our days, he will have personally gone with us.

Because in the end, it's not about us anyway. It's all about HIM.

We just get to go along for the ride.

ACKNOWLEDGMENTS

There are so many people to thank, especially those who have prayed for me during the time it's taken me to pen these words. You know who you are. I appreciate your prayers and confidence in me more than I can express. Special thanks goes to Lisa Stoltz, who I counted on throughout this process to faithfully keep my name and this project lifted to the Lord.

This book may not exist, nor my ministerial journey, were it not for Rev. Dr. Chuck Gates, who first recognized God's call on my life, pointed me in the right direction, and invested himself in me as a mentor, friend and brother. There aren't enough words to thank you.

My first book writing has been enriched by skillful guidance from Jeanette DiLouie of Innovative Editing. Her ongoing belief both in me and in the importance of the message I wanted to convey was invaluable. My thoughts and words would not have connected so well without her help. Find Jeanette at www.innovativeediting.com.

Thanks to my colleague and brother in Christ, Rev. Byron Hannon, who did a thorough advance reading for me and offered amazing insights that clarified, challenged and finessed my work. Check out Byron's blog at www.just1voice.org.

To longtime friend and colleague, Rev. Dr. Bryan Todd, who listened to my ideas for the cover and took the photo for me just for fun. What a guy! Your friendship is a blessing.

To my sister in Christ, Rev. Basha Zackavich, who contributed final layout, editing and artistic guidance. How thankful I am for your friendship. Thank you!

To Kari Tumminia, the artist who designed the cover. I am so glad we finally had the opportunity to collaborate on a project together!

And to my awesome husband, Ron, who listened to my rewrites over and over and always offered me good, honest critiques. Your patience has been a source of joy and comfort for me. There is no way I would have finished without your encouragement to keep going.

Thank you, Lord, for surrounding me with these people – I am so blessed! And thank you for putting the words on my heart to write. May all the glory go to You.

ABOUT THE AUTHOR

Rev. Shirley Goodman is an ordained elder in the Church of the Nazarene who has served in pastoral ministry for over 25 years in Philadelphia, Pennsylvania and southern New Jersey.

She loves people, and especially enjoys helping others discover ideas and truths from God's Word that can be applied to their everyday life. She is also an avid learner who consumes multi-topic podcasts and audio books while driving – and she drives a lot!

She loves music, dark chocolate and one good cup of coffee a day.

Her motivation to preach and teach is grounded by her philosophy of ministry, which she wrote in 1994 and still believes today:

> "People with a passion for the heart of God have the power to change their world toward God. This passion and power transcend race, culture, social position, economic standing, and geography. God can use anyone to advance his kingdom."

Shirley holds a B.A. in Organizational Management and an M.A. in Organizational Leadership from Eastern University in St. Davids, PA. She is married to Ron, and they have three children, five grandchildren and two great-grandchildren.

NOTES

Chapter 1

[1] Merriam Webster Dictionary online. www.merriam-webster.com

[2] Allen, Bob. "The 'Billy Graham Rule' and Women in Ministry." *Baptist News Global,* Apr. 6, 2017. www.baptistnews.com.

Chapter 2

[1] *What Paul Really Said About Women* by John Temple Bristow is quick to read, concise in thought, and helpful for those who want to learn more about women in ministerial leadership. Harperone 1988.

[2] Johnson, Alan F. General Editor. *How I Changed My Mind About Women in Leadership: Compelling Stories from Prominent Evangelicals.* Zondervan, 2010. p. 35.

[3] Ibid., 45. L.E. Maxwell, quoted in Richard Kroeger and Catherine Clark Kroeger, *I Suffer Not A Woman.* Baker, 1992. p. 33.

[4] Ps. 119:11 (NIV)

Chapter 5

[1] Weems, Lovett H. Jr. *The Journey From Readiness to Effectiveness: An Ongoing Survey of the Probationary Process in The United Methodist Church,* Second Edition (2005), p. 2. www.churchleadership.com/wp-content/uploads/2015/06/Journey _Readiness2Effect.pdf.

[2] Visit the Wesleyan Holiness Digital Library at **www.whdl.org** to access this free, multidisciplinary, open access digital resource. The library includes books, literature, multimedia material and archives in a single, repository. Content is available in multiple languages.

[3] Johnson, Alan F. General Editor. *How I Changed My Mind About Women in Leadership: Compelling Stories from Prominent Evangelicals.* Zondervan, 2010. p. 93.

Chapter 6

[1] Walker, Mark O. *The Pastor As Mentor: Creating a Culture of Mentoring in the Michigan District*: A Pastoral Research Project Submitted to the Library of Nazarene Theological Seminary; Doctor of Ministry Program, Lansing, MI. May 7, 2017.

[2] Carmichael, Evan. *Your One Word: The Powerful Secret to Creating a Business and Life that Matter.* TarcherPerigee, 2016. p. 208.

Chapter 7

[1] McLaren, Brian D. *A New Kind of Christian.* Jossey-Bass, 2001. p. 14.

[2] Espinosa, Eddie. *Change My Heart, O God.* Mercy/Vineyard Publishing. 1982.

3   Alvin Toffler - 1928-2016 American writer, futurist, and businessman known for his works discussing modern technologies including the digital revolution and the communication revolution, with emphasis on their effects on cultures worldwide.

4   Scott, Halee Gray. "Study: Female Pastors Are on the Rise." *Christianity Today.* www.Christianity Today.com/women/2017/study-female-pastors-are-on-the-rise.html. Posted Feb. 26, 2107.

Chapter 8

1   The presenters cited the works of Nancy Hedburg and Millard Erickson, two scholars among many who have written on this topic in depth. Since I have not personally read either of their works in their entirety, I've opted to use my own language here to express what I learned from the workshop.

2   Henderson, Jim. *The Resignation of Eve: What If Adam's Rib is No Longer Willing to Be the Church's Backbone?* Barna Books, 2012. pp. 119, 122

Chapter 9

1   Kreamer, Anne. *It's Always Personal: Emotion in the New Workplace.* Bedoozled, Inc. 2011. p. 134

2   Kreamer, Anne. *It's Always Personal: Emotion in the New Workplace.* Bedoozled, Inc. 2011.

3   Ibid. p. 30-31.

4   Ibid. p. 137.

5   Ibid. p. 133. Quoted from Stephanie A. Shields, *Speaking From The Heart: Gender and the Social Meaning of Emotion.* Cambridge, UK: Cambridge UP, 2002.

6   Paul, Mary Rearick. *Women Who Lead: The Call of Women in Ministry.* Beacon Hill Press, 2011. p. 41

7   Johnson, Brad W. & David Smith. *Athena Rising: How and Why Men Should Mentor Women.* Bibliomotion, Inc. 2016. pp. 93-94

8   Kreamer. p. 145.

Chapter 10

1   Brown, Brené. *I Thought I Was Just Me: Women Reclaiming Power and Courage in a Culture of Shame.* Gotham Books, Feb. 2007. www.goodreads.com/book/show/279308.I_Thought_It_Was_Just_Me

2   Goleman, Daniel. *Emotional Intelligence.* Bantam Books, 1995. p. 46.

3   Ibid. p. 315. Notes: Chapter 4, #1.

4   Goleman, Daniel. *Women Leaders Get Results: The Data.* Mar. 8, 2016. www.danielgoleman/info/women-leaders-get-results-the-data.

5   Ibid.

6 Bradberry, Travis & Jean Greaves. *Emotional Intelligence 2.0.* TalentSmart, 2009.

7 www.goodreads.com/author/quotes/14635.Robert_McCloskey

8 Brown, Brené. *The Gifts of Imperfection.* Hazelden, 2010. p. 56

9 www.gallupstrengthscenter.com

Chapter 11

1 Pastor Teddy Parker, "Facing Your Storm With Confidence" (Revival 1 of 3). YouTube.com.

2 Chan, Katie. "Pastor Teddy Parker Who Committed Suicide Struggled with Mental Illness; Memorial Service Set for Nov. 16." *Gospel Herald.* www.news@gospelherald.com. Posted Nov. 15, 2013.

3 Ibid.

Chapter 12

1 Borger, Stephen. "The Minister as a Lifelong Learner." *Grace & Peace Magazine,* Summer 2018. p. 26. www.graceandpeacemagazine.org.

2 www.sleepfoundation.org/sleepnews/do-women-need-more-sleep-than-men? Citing the work of Professor Jim Horne, director of the Sleep Research Centre at Loughborough University and author of *Sleepfaring: A Journey Through The Science Of Sleep.*

Chapter 14

1 Tannen, Deborah. *You're Wearing That? Understanding Mothers and Daughters in Conversation.* Ballantine Books, 2006. p. 12.

Epilogue

1 Brown, Brené. *Rising Strong: The Reckoning, The Rumble, The Revolution.* Spiegel & Grau, 2015. p. 110.

2 Exod. 33:12-13, New Living Translation, 2nd Ed. Tyndale House Publishers, Inc., 2004.

3 Ibid. Exod. 33:14.

44925928R00106

Made in the USA
Middletown, DE
11 May 2019